SUPER HE

Other books by Christian Godefroy

The Complete Time Management System (with John Clark)
The PowerTalk System (with Stephanie Barrat)
The Successful Negotiator (with Luis Robert)
La Dynamique Mentale
S'aider soi-même par L'Auto-hypnose
Guérison Holistique et Contrôle Cérébral
Méthode Alpha de Relaxation à Domicile
Comment Développer une Étonnante Mémoire
Développement Personnel
La Practique du Contrôle Mental

SUPER HEALTH

How to Control Your Body's Natural Defences

CHRISTIAN H. GODEFROY

PIATKUS

© 1992 Christian H Godefroy and
Edi Inter, S.A., Geneva, Switzerland

First published in 1992 by
Judy Piatkus (Publishers) Ltd of
5 Windmill Street, London W1P 1HF

First paperback edition 1993

Edited by Esther Jagger
Designed by Paul Saunders
Cover design by Jennie Smith

*A catalogue record for this book is
available from the British Library*

ISBN 0 7499 1119 0
      0 7499 1220 0 (pbk)

Typeset in 11/13pt Linotron Sabon by
Phoenix Photosetting, Chatham
Printed and bound in Great Britain by
Butler & Tanner Ltd, Frome and London

Contents

Introduction – You Are Your Own Best Doctor

When I asked Dr [Albert] Schweitzer how he explained the fact that witch doctors could cure people, he told me that I was asking him to divulge a secret that has been well kept by doctors since the time of Hippocrates.

'I'm going to tell you anyway,' he continued, his face lighting up with a smile. 'The success that the witch doctors have is due to the same reasons we are successful. Every sick person carries their own doctor around inside of them. They come to us because they don't know this fact. The best we can do is give that inner doctor a chance to act on the disease.'

Professor Norman Cousins, *The Will to Be Cured*

What would you say if someone told you that you have the power to heal?

You would probably reply: 'That's ridiculous. Only doctors, and certain people with special gifts, can heal people.' You are wrong. The truth is that we all possess the power to heal both ourselves and others. That statement is not intended to underrate the importance of diagnosticians and scientific intervention. Nor does it deny evidence that some people are gifted with extraordinary healing powers. What is meant is that there is a consensus today which recognizes the patient as the primary instrument of his or her own recovery.

This idea is based on the principle that it is impossible to separate our physical health from our psychological, emotional and spiritual wellbeing. The appearance of any physical disorder should lead us to search through our minds for the corresponding psychological problem. Illness is undeniably a message that we are sending from our mind to our physical system. In order to get better, we have to rediscover the balance and harmony of that system.

Body and Mind: in Constant Interaction

Body and mind are constantly sending messages back and forth. Our bodies are receptive to stimuli, which are then sent to the brain to be sorted out and finally returned to the body to incite movement or some other process. You can find endless examples of this interaction in your day-to-day life. Haven't you ever said: 'Oh God, I've got heartburn from last night's casserole . . .' or 'It must be the dentist's bill that's worrying me . . .'?

One of the clearest examples of mind–body interaction gone haywire is migraine headaches, which will be talked about in detail later. Migraines are absolutely harmless, yet cause inexpressible suffering. If you analyse the circumstances which lead up to a migraine attack, you may be surprised to notice that 75 per cent of the time it results from situations you would like to avoid: a party you don't want to go to, a presentation you aren't prepared to make, or a family reunion that might unearth old animosities.

A psychologist friend of mine, herself a victim of migraines, thought long and hard about the problem. She explained the phenomenon this way: 'What happens is that our brain decides to extricate us from the situation we find troublesome or embarrassing. It signals our body, which obliges by sending messages of pain.'

You are Your Own Master

We could say that our whole life either is or is not a breeding ground for disease. *Super Health* is based on the following principle: *Whether an organism functions well or is plagued with problems depends directly on the way the individual reacts to life, either by grabbing hold and directing it, or by submitting to it.*

So we are responsible for a good part, if not all, of what happens to our organism during our lifetime. Maybe you knew this already, but, like most people, you may have still preferred to rely on the inconstancies of chance, of some kind of bad luck or divine punishment, to explain away your problems.

By analysing the way in which we approach life, either controlling or submitting to it, we hold the key to good health. We just have to learn how to use it. You have undoubtedly heard about people – mostly men – who, having worked hard all their lives in excellent health, suddenly found themselves depressed and bedridden, struck down by an incurable disease, shortly after their retirement. You must also have heard about spontaneous or miraculous cures. And what about those people who smoked, ate too much, drank to excess and were moody all their lives, yet who enjoy excellent health, while others who always took care of themselves become perennial victims of health problems that are sufficiently serious to prevent them enjoying life?

But don't get too excited. This doesn't mean that you can safely smoke and loll in front of the television with a beer in your hand! Nor should you pass up all sports and a healthy lifestyle. It's all a question of attitude: the way in which we perceive our health and our bodies has a considerable influence on how we react to attacks by disease, and to the effects of bad habits.

Pioneering work on attitude and mental healing has been carried out in the United States by Bernie Siegel, Associate Clinical Professor of Surgery at Yale Medical School, and Carl Simonton, Radiation Oncologist and Medical Director of the Cancer Counselling and Research Centre at Fort Worth, Texas. They have had particular success with cancer and AIDS patients, and both have written bestselling books describing their methods.

Learning how to 'visualize' has played an important part in their treatment. Take for example Simonton's breakthrough case. His patient was a B52 pilot suffering from a malign tumour of the throat. The tumour was the size of a peach and was obstructing the passage to the lungs and stomach. The disease was progressing rapidly and, realizing that radiation therapy alone would not save his patient, Dr Simonton hit on the idea of combining the radiation treatments with image-creation techniques. Having nothing to lose, the patient agreed. He learned to enter the 'alpha state' by relaxing completely and, once relaxed, he began to visualize his white blood cells as cowboys on horseback. These cowboys attacked and destroyed the cancer cells. Over a period of seven weeks the patient repeated this procedure three times a day, for 15 minutes at a time. After seven weeks a biopsy showed that his tissue structure was once again perfectly normal. He had healed himself.

It seems that even in the case of AIDS, the techniques described in this book can sometimes trigger your natural defences enough to kill the disease. Niro Markoff Asistent did just that, as you will read in Chapter 17.

However, possessing knowledge of your personal healing powers does not mean you have to ignore all the advantages offered by modern science. The techniques of suggestion contained in this book are meant to accelerate the healing process and make other methods more effective. You will find that your attitude when taking a certain medication will, to a large extent, determine its effectiveness or ineffectiveness.

The aim of my method is to open the door to mental wellbeing, to teach you, through first simple and then more complex exercises, to see life and health from a positive point of view. In the final analysis, your doctor, healer, shaman – call it whatever you like – is first and foremost **yourself**.

Changing Attitudes

Let me tell you how I became interested in personal healing. I discovered the power of mental attitude early in my professional life. Very shy, I couldn't speak in front of an audience. I became red-faced and my heart would beat so fast that I felt it would jump out of my body. But my job involved training a group of salesmen and motivating them. I had to overcome my problem.

I went to see a hypnotist, and three sessions later I was not shy any more! I spoke in front of 4000 people and trained over 6000. My most recent one-day seminar was in Paris, in front of an audience of 2500.

After my success with the hypnotist I studied self-hypnosis and mind training, and then devised my own system. My first wife, a doctor and acupuncturist, would ask me to work with some of her patients – with wonderful results. Often friends would ask me how they could use these mental exercises in order to solve their health problems.

My first book, *La Dynamique Mentale*, was published in 1975. I received so many enthusiastic letters that I wrote *S'aider soi-même par L'Auto-hypnose* (How to Help Yourself Through Self-Hypnosis) in 1984 (*La Practique du Contrôle Mental*, 1991) and published 30 audio-tapes on self-hypnosis, visualization, relaxation, etc. When I started this work – 20 years ago – doctors would laugh at anyone who wanted to show the direct link between cancer and the mind. I remember well the first reactions when I published a tape on the subject. How things have changed!

Today, the body–mind link is well established in virtually *all* ailments. The techniques you are going to discover in this book can enhance your immune system, speed the healing process and the recovery. Try them.

PART ONE

THE BASIC
TECHNIQUES

We only make use of a minuscule part of our mental
and physical resources. Human beings live well
below their limits. They possess powers of all kinds
which they forget to use.

Professor William James

CHAPTER 1

How to Use the Powers of Your Subconscious

Years ago, before circus performers started using safety nets, there was a tightrope walker who was famous for his dangerous acrobatic feats and the awe he inspired in his audiences. He had complete confidence in himself. He knew exactly how to eliminate any trace of the fear that he surely must have felt from time to time.

Then one day a member of his family, also a circus performer, died during a show. From that moment on, the tightrope walker was struck with stage fright, with fear. Maybe he suddenly felt vulnerable, maybe he became aware of his own mortality, of the fact that, despite his prowess, he was still a member of the human race. He lost his masterful touch, and shortly afterwards was himself the victim of a fatal accident.

How can this be explained?

The Power of Our Subconscious

Our subconscious can be compared to a plot of earth where all kinds of seeds fall. The seeds are our thoughts, and most of them take root.

Positive thoughts help us deal with difficult situations: assuming our responsibilities, enjoying life, maintaining our physical and mental wellbeing. Unfortunately, it's not only the positive thoughts that penetrate through to the subconscious. Some are negative, and can become very destructive.

Negative thoughts infiltrate our minds like poison. They can cause nightmares. They can change our perception of life into something gloomy and dark, and make us easy prey for depression and anxiety. They also make us vulnerable to all kinds of pathogenic agents, since negative thoughts can weaken our immune system. And so we become ill.

Choose Your Thoughts

Our subconscious is sensitive to suggestion. It cannot sort out good thoughts from bad ones, but simply accepts them all. So it is up to you to make a conscious effort to suggest a positive direction for yourself, to plant and nourish positive seeds. You have to choose your thoughts and ideas so that what grows in the fertile soil of your subconscious is positive and results in your wellbeing.

You may have read or heard about people under hypnosis (which means that they are in direct contact with their subconscious) who have been made to create symptoms of disease. A hypnotist can persuade the subject that he or she is freezing, sweating, coughing, burning with fever and so on. This book is concerned with the inverse process. Instead of making your subconscious think that it's too cold or that you have flu, you have to convince it to regulate disorders and help you feel good.

To get back to the anecdote at the beginning of this chapter . . . as long as the tightrope walker was able to nourish his subconscious with positive thoughts, he was able to take the greatest risks with impunity. But as soon as he let the seed of fear grow in his mind, he condemned himself to failure and death.

TRY THIS EXPERIMENT

Here's a little experiment. You must know someone who always complains about their health, but who is never seriously ill.

After sharing a meal with that person, preferably something rich like seafood or a curry, pretend that you feel a little sick. You can pat your stomach, roll your eyes and moan a little. But make sure that your companion thinks it's the meal that is causing your discomfort. It will be extremely surprising if, after a few moments, he or she does not start complaining too . . . 'I don't feel too good . . . I feel bilious. . . .'

You have just seen the subconscious at work. You planted a suggestion which convinced the other person that he or she had eaten something bad or to which they were allergic. The subconscious did the rest, and the person experienced physical discomfort. It's not a question of lying or inventing – the sensation of discomfort is real enough.

The moral of all this is that you must learn to make constructive suggestions and tame your subconscious mind.

Miracles

Everyone has heard about the miracle cures that take place at Lourdes in France. It is undeniable that people with serious illnesses, some considered incurable, have been healed there. How is this possible?

In reality it isn't the holy water of Lourdes that relieves suffering or cures the sick, but the supplicant's own subconscious which accepts suggestions formed by their deep faith. They accept the idea of their recovery. They take their recovery for granted. They *visualize themselves* cured. The subconscious responds by activating its curative powers. Whether you have faith in your doctor, in certain remedies or in a divinity, it is that faith that will heal you, just as it has healed so many others throughout the ages.

Dr Alexis Carrell conducted a study of the miraculous cures documented by the Lourdes Medical Bureau, and noticed the following pattern:

> Often the subject experienced an acute pain, and then a sudden sensation of having been cured. The visible wounds tended to heal in a normal way, except at a very fast rate. *The miracle appeared to be chiefly characterized by an extreme acceleration of the normal processes of organic repair.* In a few seconds, a few minutes, or at most a few hours, wounds closed up, and all general symptoms disappeared. Appetite returned to normal. Sometimes the functional disorder disappeared before anatomical recovery. Bone deformities like Pott's disease, or cancerous growths persisted for two or three days after the healing had taken place.
>
> Dr Alexis Carrell, *Unknown Man*

In Chapter 2, you will find methods to prevent your subconscious from drowning in negative thoughts. It's just a question of making a few simple suggestions, or, if you prefer something more philosophical, of changing your attitude to life.

The Magic of Visualization

The language of the subconscious is, above all, imagination in the literal sense of the word: 'creation of images'. To tame the subconscious, to be able to make suggestions that are in tune with your desires, you first have to learn to speak its language – the language of mental imagery.

Images do not have to be visual. They can be tactile, olfactory or auditory. You probably have certain smells or tastes from your childhood that bring back a multitude of memories. Our subconscious can be trained. It's just like one of Pavlov's dogs: it gets used to reacting to a given sensation – a sound or an image or a taste. Haven't you ever started to salivate while reading a passage in a book about a sumptuous banquet? Of course you have. Sexual arousal caused by looking at an erotic or suggestive image is a perfect example of how the subconscious can affect the body directly. It's exactly this capacity for direct physical reaction that advertisers try to exploit. By creating a slogan that evokes certain images, they condition our subconscious to react automatically to a product.

So there's nothing to prevent you from consciously cultivating the ability of talking to your subconscious, and of transmitting your messages of happiness, health and serenity.

Here's an example of the power of the subconscious as proved by a scientific experiment concerning white blood cells, the 'soldiers' of the immune system:

We trained two groups of students in specific images. One group was trained to imagine neutrophils, and were told of their location and function. Another group imagined T-cells. Both T-cells and neutrophils are white blood cells, borne in bone marrow. The group that learned the neutrophil imagery had significant changes in neutrophils (but T-cells remained unchanged). The group that learned to image T-cells had significant changes in numbers of T-cells, and their neutrophils remained unchanged. These are very peculiar and highly suggestive findings.

Professor J. Achterberg, *Imagery in Healing*

How to Visualize

Objects are easier to imagine than people. As for the person who is most difficult to visualize – you guessed it, it's yourself. So just follow the step-by-step process below of learning to visualize.

EXERCISE NO. 1: YOUR ROOM

Start by closing your eyes and recalling the arrangement of furniture in your bedroom, including as many details as you can remember – colours, textures and so on.

EXERCISE NO. 2: OBJECTS

Find a comfortable place where you will not be disturbed. Pick a time of day when you're not too tired. Sit down and relax. The less physically active you are, the easier it is to visualize.

Close your eyes. At the beginning, you will not be able to visualize with your eyes open. But little by little you will be able to visualize anywhere, any time – on the bus, in a park, at a friend's house or at home. It won't even be necessary to close your eyes.

Imagine a fruit, for example an apple. You see it, you can describe it. It is green or red or yellow – whatever you want. It can be large or very small. Now change the object. Imagine a car. Decide what make and model of car, what colour and so on. Repeat the exercise with a number of everyday objects. Make sure that you see their colours clearly.

If you find that objects appear in black and white, or shades of grey, imagine that you have a palette of colours in your hand and paint the objects the colour you want, one after the other. You can also imagine a rainbow in a dark grey sky. The colours should stand out clearly against the background. At first, choose bright colours. Then try to add tones like pastels or greys.

Once you have mastered the techniques with your eyes closed, try it with your eyes open. Don't worry if you can't do it right away. It is much more difficult to see with the mind's eye, so persevere.

EXERCISE NO. 3: PEOPLE

Once you are able to visualize objects without any problem, you can move on to people. There's a trick that can help you: it's much easier to visualize a person doing a familiar, everyday action. For example, you want to visualize a friend who likes gardening. He or she is often busy in the garden when you drop by to visit, so you're used to seeing that person at work, weeding, watering and trimming. It will be much easier to visualize that person in a garden scene, dressed in gardening clothes.

Your mental images should be perfectly clear. With no fuzziness or grain. Don't omit any details. Is the person wearing gloves? What kind of shoes? Are they holding anything – a spade or rake? If they speak, can you hear what they are saying?

Don't worry about having to start all over again a few times. To avoid getting bored, change the subject or the location. Make sure you see the colours clearly. Take your time. Don't try to see everything all at once, and remember that the images must be perfectly clear. And don't ignore the other senses. Your images should include olfactory, tactile and auditory sensations as well as visual ones.

EXERCISE NO. 4: YOURSELF

Now you can move on to the most delicate and crucial part of your training: learning to visualize yourself. You should eventually be able to visualize yourself exactly as if you were looking in a mirror. Some people have a lot of difficulty with this stage. Here's a little trick that can help you.

Place a few photographs, in which your face is clearly visible, on a table in front of you. Study them. Look at all the details of your features, your clothes, your hair, the expression in your eyes. Now close your eyes and recall them one by one. In theory, you shouldn't have too much trouble. Try to visualize yourself in an outfit that you like or that you wear a lot. Also imagine yourself doing some familiar activity.

The surroundings, too, are very important. We don't live in the clouds. To a large extent, we are who we are because of what surrounds us. In concrete terms, this means that it is preferable, and easier, to visualize yourself in a familar setting (if possible free of any unnecessary tension). For example, if you don't really like your work, then avoid visualizing yourself in your workplace. If your family life is not the most serene, then don't visualize yourself at the dinner table surrounded by yelling children. And so on.

What if Your Attempts to Visualize Fail?

Some people seem to be totally incapable of creating mental images. They believe that visualizing a simple orange is impossible, whatever instruction or advice is offered. Why?

It seems that this mental block – and that's exactly what it is – stems from a *fear* of visualization, which often results in excessive activity, which in turn makes visualizing even more difficult since activity restrains visualization. So what is there to be afraid of?

These days many people regard everything that concerns mental power with suspicion. Even if you personally do not, you might have experienced this kind of scepticism and disdain in those around you – your parents or friends. It will affect the way you think.

Or it might be another, much more personal kind of fear. Maybe you hesitate to try visualization exercises because you're afraid you might discover feelings in yourself which you'd rather didn't exist. It is normal to fear certain hidden aspects of our personality. On the other hand, a certain degree of self-knowledge is essential for taming the subconscious. And occasional 'recharging' sessions are indispensable to good health.

In the next chapter I will show you how to visualize yourself in your 'sanctuary' – a personal place of retreat which you will have chosen, furnished and decorated all in your mind. This technique, if it is repeated at least one a day, will help you to acquire the psychic force which will help you to stay healthy and to overcome illness.

CHAPTER 3

Discover Inner Peace

Find a Refuge in Your Own Mental Retreat

What do you usually do when you're tired, overworked or upset? You try to find a calm place that you like, where you can relax and regenerate your mind and body, preparing yourself for further obstacles and tests. But where exactly do you go?

Depending on your temperament and resources, this magic place could be a bedroom, an office, a studio, a library, a park bench, a beach, a river bank, a clearing in a wood, a hilltop . . . it's up to you! History and literature abound with descriptions of such places. Everyone, princes and philosophers alike, feels the need to take a 'mental break'.

But sometimes our favourite place of retreat is not accessible. We might be stuck in town, at work or travelling. Or we might have to be with other people all day – colleagues or members of our family. In short, it's impossible to get away. But if you want to communicate with your subconscious, you must be absolutely alone with yourself. How can you do this? Simply by creating a place of retreat in your mind.

Even if you can't get there physically, you can place yourself in your refuge mentally for a few minutes. Of course, if you already have a preferred place it will be easier to put yourself there in your mind. You just have to visualize it, and then imagine yourself there. If not, create the ideal refuge. Does that sound difficult? Well, it isn't, and anyone can do it.

AN UNLIMITED UNIVERSE

1. Start by defining your preferences. Would you like to retreat to a comfortable room surrounded by your favourite books, or would you prefer the seashore or a mountainside, the tower of a castle, a mysterious cave . . . anything is allowed.
2. If you think you really lack imagination, look through architecture or design magazines, or books on nature, or even tourist guides. Or look at your old holiday snaps. You're sure to find a spot you like, where you've always dreamed of living. You may decide on the quiet atmosphere of a monastery, or a little clearing under the pines, a Japanese garden, a painted landscape, an island surrounded by soft beaches . . . the choice is infinite.
3. Once you have chosen your place of refuge, set it up according to your tastes, making any changes that come to mind.
4. You can also draw it. Some of us are 'visual' and are better able to clarify things when they are down on paper. Can't draw? It doesn't matter – you'll be the only one to see it anyway!

HOW TO GET TO YOUR FAVOURITE PLACE

1. Relax yourself completely with the following technique:
   - Get comfortable, wherever you are. Don't lie down if you think you might fall asleep. Try to make sure you won't be disturbed.
   - Breathe deeply, quietly. Close your eyes.
   - First relax your face (forehead, brows, cheeks, mouth, chin); then move down to your chest, shoulders and arms. Next relax your abdomen, legs and feet. You should feel your muscles relaxing. (This step is essential, so don't leave it out.) Every time you feel a group of muscles relax, count to ten before moving on to the next ones.
   - The next step is a little more difficult. You have to relax your mind. This might take some practice. First try to let all the thoughts and ideas flow through your mind, without stopping to think about them. Don't let them disturb you. After a few moments you will notice that your mind feels light. All your thoughts have dissipated, leaving room for a marvellous feeling of serenity. Now you are ready to receive new, positive ideas.

You might fall asleep the first few times you do the relaxation exercise. Don't worry – it just means that you were very relaxed. But if you keep falling asleep, you might want to look at your sleeping habits. It's possible that you're not getting enough sleep at night, and don't have time to recuperate fully. You might be suffering from one of the many forms of insomnia. If that is the case, try to improve the quality of your sleep. Each night, before falling asleep, repeat this same exercise. You will probably find your sleeping hours much more restorative.

Now let's get back to your mental retreat.

2. You are now absolutely calm. You know that you are regenerating mentally and physically. All you have to do now is fly to your refuge.

3. Count to three, then visualize your refuge.

4. Study all the details of your ideal place. If you're in a library, breathe the odour of the books and touch the smooth leather on the chairs. If you're on the beach, feel the sand under your feet, listen to the waves, breathe the salt air. If you're in a wood or on a mountainside, fill your lungs with the smell of leaves and clean pasture. Touch the bark. Listen to the birds singing, the wind rustling the leaves overhead. If you're in a studio, pick up the objects in the room one by one. If you're in a monastery, smell the incense or the old stone walls or the wooden pews, listen to the sound of monks chanting in the chapel . . . and so on. Be aware of all the sensations emanating from the location.

5. Count slowly to ten. Breathe deeply. You feel wonderfully well in your chosen refuge. Enjoy all the beautiful detail and comfort it offers.

6. That's enough for the first 'trip'. Time to get back to your daily routine. Count slowly to ten and open your eyes.

7. You're back where you started from, but with renewed energy from your journey. You feel fine, robust and healthy. You are in harmony with the universe.

HOW TO GET THE MOST OUT OF YOUR RETREAT

It is essential that you retreat at least once a day for fifteen or twenty minutes. Consider it a daily holiday. Even if you don't place any special demands on your subconscious – if you just want to feel better – these few minutes will endow you with an enormous amount of strength and calm. In other words, it is essential that you maintain this ability to isolate yourself mentally. If you don't visit your refuge often enough, you'll forget it, and when you really need it you'll have to go through the steps all over again.

So one of the best pieces of advice I can give you is *never* to neglect spending some time each day in your place of refuge. Who knows? Some day it might save your sanity – or even your life.

CHAPTER · 4

How to Communicate with Your Subconscious

We frequently become ill because we think that illness is the unavoidable reaction to a given situation. In a manner of speaking our subconscious resolves a problem by throwing us into the lion's den of disease. It might be the only way the subconscious finds to free itself of conflict which it deems intolerable.

Your subconscious is your taskmaster. In the final analysis, it is what controls your life. But the instructions it sends to your immune system originate in your conscious mind. So, once you know how to get *into* your mental retreat and *communicate* with your subconscious, you should persist in the practice every day and establish a firm connection with your inner self. Every time you take refuge in your retreat after a few minutes of relaxation, speak to your subconscious. Send messages through your mind.

Learn the Messages that Shield Your Health

Here are a few phrases that should become your slogans. Since the subconscious needs to be conditioned, try using this bit of 'brainwashing' by repeating the phrases over and over again during the day and setting up the shields that will protect your health.

– I will prohibit negative thoughts. Everything that happens to me has a positive side.

- I will use the power of my mind to master my thoughts, and to keep my mind and body in good health.

- I will never use the power of my mind to harm others.

- In my place of refuge I am free, I am the master of my subconscious.

- There is no natural energy that is bad – it all depends how it is used.

- I will never let others think for me. I must be master of my thoughts and my actions.

- Illness starts in the mind. I will never allow myself to fall victim to thoughts that will make me ill.

- My body and mind are perfectly healthy, and they'll stay that way.

- My muscles are strong and supple.

- My heart is strong. My blood is pure.

- My digestion is good.

- I do not get depressed.

- I am slim and in good shape.

Of course, you are entirely free to create your own message-shields and to modify the ones here according to your needs; but don't forget that they should be phrased in the form of affirmations. You state positively that you will or will not do such and such a thing. Never say 'I would like' or 'If only I could . . .'. Talk to your subconscious like an employer talking to a servant. Don't let any doubts plant destructive thoughts in your mind.

Practise the Language of the Subconscious

In Chapters 1–3 you learned that the language of the subconscious is the language of images. Now is the time to put that knowledge to good use. Every time you formulate a message-shield, or affirmation, transform it into an image. Does that sound difficult? It may be easy to visualize a healthy heart, or supple, strong muscles, but it gets a little more complicated when you start dealing with pure thoughts. Let's say your message-shield is something like: 'My thoughts are more and more positive.' How can you visualize this so that your subconscious can understand?

You use what is the blackboard technique. This is a very general method, which will be used over and over again in this book. Set up in your mind the image of two blackboards, one black and one white. You should be able to call them up whenever you are in your retreat. Next to the blackboards, imagine a hammer or a mallet.

BACK TO SCHOOL – A LIBERATING EXPERIENCE

On the blackboard, write your negative thoughts. 'I may lose my job. . .', 'The bank will never let me have that overdraft. . .', 'I don't believe my partner is faithful. . .', 'I'm afraid my children are taking drugs. . .', 'I'm going to fail my exam. . .', and so on. Get all the things that are bothering you out in the open.

Write these negative thoughts on the blackboard in white chalk, just as if you were back at school, so that you can read them clearly in your mind. Once you've finished, read them over again.

Think hard about what you've just written. Breathe deeply. Now pick up the hammer or mallet and smash the blackboard into a thousand pieces! Let all your fury come out as you destroy the board. Don't hold anything back. You must *hate* the thoughts you've just formulated and destroy them completely. The angrier you are, the more you'll benefit from the execution.

Now take a few minutes to calm yourself. Breathe deeply, count to ten or twenty. Re-establish your calm. At this point you might want to recall your retreat. Build it up slowly, calmly, making sure you are completely relaxed. You should not lose the feeling of wellbeing that your retreat elicits in you.

THE BEST IDEAS ARE THE ONES THAT LAST

Now turn your attention to the white board. Pick up a blue or black felt marker, and write down your positive thoughts (generally the opposite of the negative ones you have just destroyed). For example: 'I will keep my job. . . ', 'The bank will let me have the money. . .', 'I have complete confidence in my partner. . .', 'My children are healthy and honest. . .' and so on. Don't forget that you must write only affirmations.

Now read calmly over what you've written a few times. Allow yourself to savour the feelings of power, love, warmth, confidence and honesty that your shields provide. The feeling of joyous serenity that pervades you should stay with you for good. Your subconscious, on which these images have been inscribed, will reflect them back to you in the form of new, positive behaviour.

To inscribe these message-shields deeply into your subconscious, you should repeat the process as often as possible. Not only will this exercise help maintain your mental and physical health, it will also help you start controlling your destiny.

CHAPTER 5

Recharge Your Psychic Energy Batteries

> . . . we suggest that visual imaging techniques be used as a complement to standard medical practices. These methods are especially useful before a doctor can get to the scene, or if the disorder is considered incurable.
>
> Dr Irwin Oyle, *Healing Mind*

The Luminous Sphere Method

Here is an excellent exercise to purify your body and experience new-found energy. It is preferable to do this exercise in the morning when you wake up, or at the beginning or end of a relaxation period or subconscious communication, even if you had nothing in particular to work on – it's by constantly recharging your batteries that you can best maintain your physical and mental health. Whatever the occasion, this visualization helps recharge your psychic batteries.

In time, you will learn to develop your own exercises. But for now, the luminous sphere method is essential for your psychic development. The white light represents energy, optimism, everything positive in life, beauty and bounty, honesty and confidence.

Stretch out on your back, with your arms by your sides or with your hands crossed on your chest. Close your eyes. Relax, using the technique you learned in Chapter 3. Breathe deeply from the abdomen. (see Chapter 6 for breathing techniques).

Alternatively you can sit in a comfortable chair, with your back relatively straight (don't sprawl or slouch) and your feet touching the ground. Get yourself as comfortable as possible. The main thing is to relax and to breathe calmly.

EXERCISE

1. Imagine a globe of white light floating above your head. Breathe deeply and count to ten, feeling the light shining over you.

2. Now imagine that the luminous sphere is slowly penetrating your skull and spreading into your brain. Breathe deeply and count to ten again.

3. The light now spreads down to your chest, which starts glowing softly. Breathe deeply once more, as you feel the energy of the light flowing through your veins, tingling in all your pores.

4. Now the light moves down to your solar plexus. Visualize the white sphere surrounding your sternum. Breathe deeply and count to ten.

5. Now imagine the light moving down to your hips. It fills you with light and warmth. Breathe while counting to ten.

6. The light now moves down to your legs and feet. Once again breathe deeply and count.

7. When this is done, imagine the light shining through your whole body, from the top of your head to the tips of your toes. It's like an enormous sun whose rays penetrate right to the centre of your physical being. Breathe deeply, and feel the light all around you and inside you. Visualize the cleansing energy moving up the left side of your body, and then down the right side. Continue breathing deeply.

8. Finally, imagine that the light source is in your solar plexus, spreading out from there through your whole body. Now get ready to come back to earth.

After doing this exercise, you should feel totally cleansed of the negative energies in and around you. You are full of extraordinary, positive energy. Now put it to good use!

CHAPTER 6

How to 'Breathe' Health

Now that you have mastered the elementary techniques of educating your subconscious, you can learn how to make the subconscious receptive to your every wish.

Since it was discovered that the subconscious does not differentiate between what exists in reality and what is imagined to exist with sufficient intensity, specialists in the field have worked on developing methods to maximize the intensity of imagined phenomena. These techniques depend on the body as much as the mind. They use certain latent abilities which we all possess, but which we have never had the occasion to exploit in practice.

These techniques, in order of increasing difficulty, are:

– breathing (inhalation and exhalation)

– alpha relaxation

– meditation (visualization, concentration and mantra repetition)

– self-hypnosis

They are all directly related, and can frequently be combined. The boundary between meditation and self-hypnosis is extremely vague, to the point where some specialists qualify the relationship between the two techniques by giving them another name: hypnomeditation.

The last three techniques call for total physical relaxation, during which the brain emits what are called 'alpha' waves. We'll talk more about this a little later on.

Relearning to Breathe

All living things breathe. Animals breathe, vegetables breathe. We sometimes get the impression that even certain minerals breathe. It's only an impression, but it is true that there is an exchange of energy between rocks and the environment.

Breathing is an essential element of our health. A healthy person is said to 'breathe health'. We inhale fresh pure air (at least ideally) before exhaling air polluted with the toxins produced in our organism. So with each intake of air we nourish our organs, and with each exhalation we clean them.

The brain is an organ just like the heart or the liver, and therefore benefits from healthy, controlled breathing. By relearning to breathe, you will at the same time master your vital forces and develop your psychic faculties.

In the West, breathing techniques were rediscovered only a short time ago. Here is some advice which comes to us from far back in time. Chinese doctors were teaching their patients to practise this kind of breathing when the West was just entering the Iron Age.

AVOID BREATHING THROUGH YOUR MOUTH

Breathing through the mouth is dangerous because it dries out the mucous membranes and results in infections of the mouth and larynx. Always breathe through your nose (with the exceptions described below).

When you are engaged in exercise, especially sports (running, cycling, dancing, skiing, swimming etc.) and your cardiac rhythm is accelerated for a certain time, you will be forced to breathe through your mouth. Your muscles need an extra supply of oxygen, and breathing through your nose is not enough. Also, while you are doing strenuous exercise, avoid holding air in your lungs. In other words, don't forget to breathe. If you do, your muscles will become starved of oxygen. Once your cardiac rhythm is back down to normal, start breathing through your nose again.

BREATHE WITH YOUR ABDOMEN

Chest breathing is not very useful to the organism. It might seem the most logical way to breathe, since our lungs are situated in our chest. But if you learn to breathe from your abdomen, you will quickly notice the difference. You will eliminate many more of your toxins by breathing from your abdomen.

You should feel your stomach inflate and deflate with each inhalation and exhalation of air.

BREATHE MORE DEEPLY AND LESS OFTEN

If you've ever practised an endurance sport, you will know about this energy-saving technique. For those of you who haven't, here are a few tips that will help you:

1. Get into a comfortable position.
2. Breathe in deeply, lifting your head slightly back.
3. Stop breathing for a moment. You should never hold your breath for longer than half the time it takes to inhale or exhale.
4. Breathe out fully, emptying your lungs and stomach. This is a crucial step which detoxifies your respiratory system.
5. Stop breathing for a few seconds.
6. Start again.

Try to exercise your breathing a few times a day. You can do it while you're riding on the bus or tube, for example, or driving your car, or waiting for a phone call. Try to do it for five to ten minutes every time you get the chance.

SOME BASIC TIPS ON BREATHING

- Inhaling and exhaling should take the same amount of time.
- Your breathing should be completely silent.
- While you are practising, imagine that you're breathing in health and that you are filling your body with vital energy. You are an active and dynamic person. You are overflowing with energy. Repeat these message-shields with every cycle of inhalation–exhalation.

Now for some more advanced breathing techniques.

RECITE YOUR VOWELS

Don't be alarmed – you aren't being asked to act like a child! In this technique you use your voice while exhaling, usually on a vowel. It is thought that while silent breathing has a calming effect, voiced exhalation has a curative effect on our organism. In other words, the former results in a general feeling of wellbeing, while the latter plays an active role in regulating certain disorders.

- Breathing out the letter 'A' (aaaaaaah!) relaxes your ribcage and has an overall soothing effect.
- Breathing out the letter 'E' takes care of your bronchial tubes, your throat and your vocal chords. It helps prevent angina, tonsillitis and laryngitis.
- Breathing out the letter 'I' regularizes your blood circulation. Use this vowel if you always have cold feet and hands.
- Breathing out the letter 'O' cleans your lungs, increases the efficiency of your respiration, and at the same times makes breathing easier. It is no coincidence that many traditional work songs (sung by sailors, navvies etc.) used this vowel a lot (Heave Ho!).
- Breathing out on the letter 'U' improves your digestion. Although very simple, this technique has a powerful effect. Try it and you will be pleasantly surprised.

USE YOUR HEART

It seems that if you time your breathing to the rhythm of your heartbeat, the positive effects are multiplied. Actually, it makes perfect sense since both heart and lungs are nourished by the same flow of blood.

First determine your heartbeat by taking your pulse. Do this by pressing two fingers lightly on your jugular vein, found just under your jaw on the right side, midway between the chin and the earlobe.

Once you know your heartbeat, breathe as you have just learnt, deeply and calmly. After a moment you should start feeling a pulse in your stomach.

Adopt the following rhythm:

1. Inhale for eight heartbeats
2. Hold your breath for four heartbeats
3. Exhale for eight heartbeats
4. Stop breathing for four heartbeats.

Adapt the rhythm to your own physical condition. The better shape you're in, the longer you can inhale and exhale. But the time you hold your breath should always be half that of an inhalation or exhalation.

This exercise should be done at least three times a day for ten to fifteen minutes, and is an excellent way to protect yourself against infections of the lungs and larynx. It will also help to increase your store of energy.

MAKE OTHER PARTS OF YOUR BODY BREATHE

One afternoon a machinist hurt his hand. The company doctor examined the damaged fingers and sent the worker home. That night the injured hand became very painful, and the man started moaning. His wife had just read an article about an ancient Zen technique, and half jokingly suggested he try it. The man mumbled that he didn't appreciate her suggestion. He took a few aspirins but they didn't help. As the night wore on, the pain became intolerable. In desperation, he asked his wife to tell him about the Zen technique . . . 'I'll try anything!'

She explained that when young Zen monks had an itch or a pain, they were taught to repeat a kind of chant that corresponded to the problem ('Pain . . . pain . . . pain?) and instead of trying to ignore the problem, to immerse themselves in it.

The machinist tried the technique. Here's what happened, as reported by the man himself: 'I spoke to my damn fingers like I was speaking to a gang of dirty kids. I started to appreciate the quality of the pain. I concentrated all my attention on it. And then, suddenly Bang! It was gone! Like I'd turned off a switch.'

Marilyn Ferguson, *The Brain Revolution*

This is not a joke. Everything in this method is absolutely serious. You have already learnt how to imagine, how to visualize just about any-thing, and it is precisely through these breathing techniques that you can make your organs and limbs breathe.

Get comfortable. You can, for example, take refuge in your mental retreat. If not, any place that is comfortable and where you won't be disturbed will do.

Say you have a toothache. With each breath, imagine that your tooth is breathing also and that it is being purified. After a short time you should feel a sensation of heat in the painful part of your body, in this case your tooth. A little later, if you continue the breathing exer-cise, the feeling of warmth will be replaced by one of cold. After some minutes you are certain to experience a diminishing of pain. Do the exercise for at least fifteen minutes.

You can soothe pain in any part of your body in this way. But if the pain returns after you stop, despite your efforts to control it, and especially if you're not aware of its cause, consult a doctor.

The technique can be used very effectively against migraines, which so many people suffer from. Or if you've just had an operation, the exercise will allow you to control your blood circulation and accelerate healing.

CHAPTER 7

Alpha Relaxation Techniques

First, it would be wise to explain what alpha waves are, since they have been the subject of so much literature and discussion since their discovery at the turn of this century.

What are Alpha Waves?

An electroencephalogram or EEG, is the traditional way doctors measure the activity of our brain cells. Apparently this activity has a very definite structure. The EEG detects four main types of brain waves:

- alpha waves, which correspond to extremely reduced brain activity, deprived of sensory stimulation, are produced in a state half way between sleep and waking
- beta waves are produced when the brain is fully awake, and correspond to a state of concentrated awareness
- theta waves are produced during some phases of sleep
- delta waves occur during deep sleep or in a semi-comatose state.

What Characterizes the Alpha State?

You will have heard about magicians who lie on a bed of nails, of Tibetan yogis who can sit naked in the coldest Himalayan weather, and of certain cultures which incorporate walking on fire as part of their initiation rites. These feats are, it seems, performed while in the alpha state. But don't worry – you don't have to walk on fire or sit naked in the snow (although you can try it if you like)!

It's very simple: relaxation creates alpha waves. You just have to relax, gaze into space as you sit comfortably, letting your thoughts flow without trying to retain them, in order to produce alpha waves. The moment you close your eyes, you automatically produce a burst of alpha waves.

Repetitive actions are especially conducive to producing alpha waves. You might start doing a breathing exercise, or repeat a word or phrase, or concentrate on an object that moves in a regular rhythm, silently or with sound (pendulum, metronome etc.).

Just think about how a regular, soft sound can put you to sleep. . . .

The Alpha Method: A Goldmine of Energy

The alpha method consists of several steps which can be divided into three general stages.

The first involves entering the alpha state through concentration. The second reinforces the relaxed state through precise suggestions. You can, if you wish, stop here and benefit from the few moments of total relaxation. But you can also go on to train your subconscious by repeating the message-shields that you have learnt.

FIRST STAGE

1. Get comfortable, either in your mental retreat or in a dimly lit, quiet room.

2. Loosen or remove any clothing that might restrain you. You must be perfectly comfortable.

3. Keep your eyes open and stare at a point in front of you. Concentrate on this point and study it in detail. Do not let your gaze wander.

4. Now close your eyes. As you do this, you should feel a deep sense of relaxation. Your body feels good, and your eyes muscles are relaxed.

5. Do a few of the breathing exercises you learned in Chapter 6.

SECOND STAGE

6. Begin by staring at a point in front of you, and then closing your eyes. Feel the alpha waves flooding your brain. Repeat this a number of times, until you really feel the effects produced by closing your eyes.

7. One after the other, tighten each of your muscles and then relax them. Start with the feet, then move up to the legs, thighs, buttocks, stomach, arms, shoulders, neck, face. Tighten each muscle as much as possible – until it hurts – and keep it tight for a few seconds before releasing it. This process should take at least five minutes.

8. When you have finished tightening and loosening all your muscles, experience the deep feeling of relaxation for a few minutes. It's as if you're floating – your body is weightless, without sensation, as light as a feather or a cloud.

9. Now tell yourself that one of your arms is getting heavier. You feel the heaviness. It weighs more and more. When you arm feels like a ton of lead, move on to the other arm and then to your legs. You should feel the heaviness of your limbs. You are to all intents and purposes stuck to your chair or bed.

THIRD STAGE

10. Now formulate your message-shields and impress them on your subconscious. Be clear, brief and affirmative.

11. To awaken completely, flex your joints for a few minutes before opening your eyes. Your body feels light, blood is pumping strongly through your veins, and you slowly regain consciousness of the exterior world.

12. Open your eyes. You feel great. You have just replenished your storehouse of energy, and at the same time you have gained more control over your destiny.

The relaxation method you have just learnt will become a beneficial tool in your everyday life. I refer to it as the 'flexing' exercise. Not only will it help you neutralize the negative effects of stress, psychological tension and all the problems you have to deal with, it will also become your guarantee of health, happiness and wellbeing – the tool for success in life.

CHAPTER 8

Meditation That Heals

An Innate Ability

Ancient civilizations were aware that meditation could cure many illnesses. Unfortunately, through the ages we have come to believe that only the most gifted mystics are able to practise techniques of meditation that have a positive effect on health. But that simply isn't true.

For example, in ancient times, healer-priests surrounded their meditation sessions with a host of rituals that were incomprehensible to the uninitiated. They probably did this to preserve an aura of magic in order to maintain their following – they had to earn a living like everybody else! If the common people had realized just how much the wool was being pulled over their eyes, these great civilizations, founded on religion, would have crumbled a lot sooner.

In reality, there is absolutely nothing magic about meditation techniques, and anyone can do them.

What Can it do for You?

You already know that meditation can help you relax. It allows you to externalize the tensions that are bothering you. Secondly, it forces you to observe and question your acts, words and feelings, and enables you to discover the hidden causes behind them. It is most probable that this kind of examination of your consciousness (all religious connotation excluded) will help you steer your way more easily through life. Last, and most important, meditation can heal, or at least soothe, disease. And that's what we're mainly concerned with in this book.

Every time you meditate your blood vessels dilate, your pulse slows down, your breathing becomes regular and your blood pressure lowers. So it is safe to say that meditation has some of the same beneficial effects on the organism as physical exercise.

It also seems true, according to researchers, that two daily meditation sessions of fifteen minutes each have the same effect on our organism as two hours sleep. During meditation the brain emits alpha waves, which puts us into a state of deep relaxation without losing consciousness.

It has been discovered that two meditation sessions per day produce these concrete results:

- lowered blood pressure
- prevention of asthma attacks and sinusitis
- prevention of migraines
- prevention of ulcers
- prevention of insomnia
- prevention of depression

A pretty good list, don't you think? And these aren't the only positive effects of meditation. It's worth a try, isn't it?

How to Meditate through Visualization

There are many forms of therapeutic and protective meditation, but the simplest ones are often the best.

The basis of the first meditation technique here is visualization. You have learnt how to visualize, and you are practising regularly in your mental retreat.

Start with a very simple, very concrete exercise.

MEDITATION: A WALK IN NATURE

Imagine that you're walking in the country on a superb October day. Birds chirp in the trees, golden leaves float gently on the wind. The sun is warm on your back. A golden light shines over the countryside. You smell the dried leaves underfoot and the fresh scent of pines. You stop near a little brook, glittering in the sunshine. Tiny minnows swim in the crystal-clear water. Crickets chirp in the fields. You are filled with a sense of wellbeing, happiness and tranquillity.

Now open your eyes and feel the warmth that has spread through your body. You feel calm, relaxed, rested. Everything is right in the world.

Of course, you are entirely free to modify and improve this visualization. You can create any other scenes which you think will have the same effect on you. The important thing is to include as many details as possible – images of smell, touch, taste and sound as well as sight.

To Control Healing Energy

This exercise is a little more complex, and demands a good understanding of the three techniques you have already learnt: relaxation, breathing and visualization.

1. Get comfortable in your mental retreat and relax. Start with the feet and work up the entire length of your body to the crown of the skull.

2. Feel your muscles expand and your joints relax.

3. Enjoy the feeling of wellbeing.

4. Now relax your mind as you have learnt to do, by letting your thoughts flow without trying to follow them or prevent them from appearing. Your brain will soon be in the alpha state.

5. If you like, you can start with the 'luminous sphere' exercise (p. 30) and fill yourself with renewed psychic energy.

6. Now imagine a golden light all round you, a kind of luminous aura that surrounds your entire body. Feel it, breathe it, touch it.

7. Ask yourself if there's anything in your life that needs changing, or if you feel pain in any part of your body.

8. If you succeed in defining your problem, keep it fixed in your mind. If by chance everything is going well in your life, continue with the exercise anyway, and it will have a protective effect rather than a therapeutic one.

9. Now imagine the healing energy settling in the part of your body that is painful or sick. Visualize it penetrating your body to soothe and heal you.

10. If your problem is not physical but moral, face it head on! Concentrate on it and explore it from all sides. Get to the root of the problem while continuing to imagine yourself surrounded by golden light.

This exercise is especially effective if you have the impression that others are controlling and directing your life. It will teach you to sound out the innermost depths of your subconscious and to understand why you let yourself be manipulated so easily. In other words, it will get rid of your negative thoughts which, as you now know, are often the cause of physical ailments, both minor and serious.

Once you have accomplished this stage, imagine yourself completely healthy, happy, shining with energy and enthusiasm. Everything is working out for the best in your life.

Imagine yourself overflowing with love. Repeat your message-shields:

- I am in excellent health. I am full of energy.
- I can direct my life as I wish.
- I am in perfect harmony with the universe.
- I am completely happy.
- Everything I do succeeds.

Concrete Image Meditation

This more advanced technique is very popular among numerous schools of mysticism in the East. It consists of staring at an object without allowing your mind to use words to describe it. Usually an organic object like a shell or a leaf is used, and you look at it as if you were touching it with your eyes.

Sounds difficult? It's true that this kind of meditation is more complex than the ones you've learnt up to now. But don't worry. If you've managed everything in the book up to now, you won't have any trouble going further.

To understand how it works, an example might be useful. Take a piece of clothing made from velvet or satin. Place it next to you and run your fingers lightly over a small area of the fabric for about half a minute. Now look at the same piece of material. Study it. For most of us, these two kinds of perceptions are different. When we touch something, we don't usually need words to describe the sensation. On the other hand, visual sensation seems to necessitate words.

The aim of concrete image meditation is to develop the ability to look at an object exactly as if you were touching it, without resorting to words to describe the sensation.

Place an object in front of you (a stone, leaf, shell, egg etc.) and look at it. You will probably have difficulty concentrating on the object. You will feel like moving, looking somewhere else. You will want to use words to describe your visual perception. You'll suddenly think of something that's been bothering you for a few days. In short, you will not be able to discipline your mind.

Place the object at a comfortable distance. Generally, the distance you hold a book from your eyes when reading is best. Look at the whole object. Don't concentrate on a particular point. Constantly relax your gaze. You might start to have optical illusions. You will get the impression that the object is moving, either closer or further away, or that it's surrounded by a glowing light, or that it's shrinking or expanding.

Don't worry – this is all very natural. These phenomena are explained by the brain's desire to escape from the discipline you are imposing on it. Some people even get the feeling that they're the ones who are moving, and not the object.

PRACTICAL ADVICE

Force yourself to demystify these kinds of illusions. Recognize them for what they are, and don't let them manipulate you. They really are only in your mind, and do not exist externally.

You should do this exercise for at least ten minutes a day. After a few weeks, start making your sessions longer, adding a few minutes at a time. After a month, you should be concentrating for twenty minutes. Afterwards it's up to you whether or not you want to prolong your sessions. Don't overtire yourself, and don't try to go too fast.

Here are a few tips that should make learning concrete image meditation easier:

- If possible, use the same object for a number of sessions. You will progress more quickly.
- Flowers are not recommended as an object of meditation. It is easy to fall into a kind of subliminal trance when contemplating a flower.
- Also avoid objects which have a symbolic value, either personal or popular (a candle, cross, rosary etc.). This will slow your progress.

- Finally, the simplest objects are the best. If you don't want to use something organic or natural, you can use a piece of material of solid colour, or a rough jewel that isn't too big.

Don't expect 100 per cent success each time. Sometimes it might just not work. Don't force it – stop and begin again the next day.

Meditation through Mantra Repetition

A mantra is a group of sounds that are repeated. They can be sounds taken from nature, like the sound of a waterfall; they can be musical notes; or even sounds without any precise origin or meaning.

Some schools of meditation prefer using meaningful phrases or a refrain, often taken from a hymn or psalm, for example *Kyrie Eleison*. Some experts suggest that the phrase should have seven syllables. The only explanation of this is the mystical connotation often given to the number seven by many cultures, expecially oriental ones.

What you must understand at this point is that the value of the mantra itself is purely symbolic. The sound of it should be pleasant and inoffensive, so that you can enter the alpha state without disturbance.

Experts in mantra meditation are divided as to why it works. One reliable school claims that it is the vibratory effect of repeating the mantra that resonates in certain parts of the body and in certain organs. As yet, there is no scientific proof that this is true.

CHOOSE A PERSONAL MANTRA

One thing is certain: even though we don't know exactly how mantra repetition works, there is no doubt that it *does* work. So you should include it in your series of meditation exercises.

The constant repetition of a mantra, combined with the regular deep breathing of a relaxation session, aims to break the usual 'moulds' or patterns of our thoughts, so that new, positive ones can take their place. Practitioners claim that once the new thoughts are installed we lose interest in the old ones, which then fade away.

How do you choose a mantra? Theories on this subject abound. One that makes a lot of sense is a simple technique developed by Dr Lawrence LeShan, a New York psychologist and a specialist on meditation. His book *How to Meditate* earned him worldwide recognition.

Dr LeShan claims it's best to choose a group of sounds which have no meaning, and which are relatively short (two to three syllables). He suggests opening your telephone directory and placing your index finger anywhere on the page. Use the first syllable of the name you have randomly chosen. Then turn to another page and do the same thing. You've got your mantra.

What next?

DETACH YOURSELF FROM YOUR SURROUNDINGS

Here are the steps you should follow to become adept at mantra meditation:

1. Get comfortable.

2. Spend a few minutes relaxing, using the technique you learnt earlier. Do a few breathing exercises.

3. Start to chant your mantra. A few precautions to consider:

   – You should chant out loud, but keep the sound barely audible so as not to dry out the mucous membranes in your mouth.

   – Also some people who are susceptible to hyperventilation (notably smokers) might get dizzy from chanting too loudly.

4. Try to avoid distractions while repeating the mantra. Find the rhythm you're comfortable with and stick to it.

5. Start with fifteen-minute sessions. After some weeks extend them, if you feel you are really benefiting from the practice.

6. Practise for two or three weeks before making this type of meditation a part of your regular programme.

Not everyone likes to do mantra meditation. Although most schools of mysticism approve of the practice, claiming it to be as effective as any other form of meditation, there are some people who find it tiresome or boring. But if you get to the point where you can concentrate completely on your chanting and block out everything around you except the mantra, then you will have achieved your aim.

How Can You Tell if You are Meditating?

Even after you start meditating, thoughts keep rolling through your mind. Just let them be. Noises from the outside might seem louder.

Don't let them bother you. Ignore them. Concentrate on the rhythms of your body: your breathing, your heartbeat. You will feel detached from everything going on around you.

It's possible you could start feeling some heat in your arms and legs. You might also stop feeling the surface on which you are sitting or lying. Once everything around you has 'disappeared', once you have lost your sense of time and your thoughts have stopped, you have attained the transcendental state.

When you return to earth, you will feel all your senses heightened. You will feel refreshed and relaxed, as if you've just taken a revitalizing nap. A successful session of meditation will greatly replenish your store of energy.

CHAPTER · 9

How to Control Your Body through Self-hypnosis

What is Hypnosis?

The ability of our subconscious to control a physiological or physical function (even if it is imperceptible) is, without doubt, one of the most prodigious faculties of the human mind – and also one of the most overlooked.

Dr Barbara Brown, *Supermind: The Ultimate Energy*

Even today this simple term is shrouded in a thick veil of mystery. For many people, hypnosis is not entirely reputable. It scares us, evoking strange powers wielded by beings who are a little threatening, and who may make us involuntarily relinquish control of our will.

But in reality, hypnosis is nothing more than one of the states of consciousness between complete awareness and sleep. All human beings, and numerous species of animals, can experience the hypnotic state.

Hypnotic trance has been with us since the dawn of history. Practically all civilizations used it for one reason or another, especially for medical purposes. And it is while we are in this intermediate state that our subconscious is most open to suggestion.

A Question of Sensitivity

Under hypnosis we feel things intensely and can effortlessly imagine sensations such as relaxation, sleepiness, softening or hardening of muscles, heat or cold and so on. These sensations can sometimes be extreme, as the following example demonstrates.

A few years ago in France a Dr Platonov was researching into hypnosis and its therapeutic possibilities and asked a well-known hypnotist (N. I. Finne) to put one of his patients 'under' in his presence, and to make certain suggestions.

The hypnotist suggested to the patient, after she had been hypnotized, that she was going to be branded with a red-hot iron. Then, using a glass tube dipped in cold water, the doctor lightly touched the patient's arm. It sounds incredible, but not only did the patient scream out in pain when touched with the cold tube, she also developed a sizeable burn mark, surrounded by blisters, which appeared almost immediately.

Here's another story, a little more amusing. In the sixties, on a televised demonstration of hypnotism which was being broadcast live from a studio, the hypnotist decided to suggest to his four subjects that they were in the middle of the desert, dying of heat and thirst. It worked so well that the subjects started undressing to cool themselves off, and the hypnotist had to make another, very rapid suggestion to prevent one of the women from ending up stark naked in front of the cameras!

The Mental and Physical Characteristics of the Hypnotic State

These characteristics are innumerable and sometimes very subtle. Here is a short list of the ones that are most easily recognizable:

- Your eyes are closed.
- Your body is totally relaxed, and your breathing slows down.
- You are unconscious of what is going on around you.
- On the other hand, you are much more aware of your internal functions, such as pulse and respiratory rhythm.
- Your sensory awareness is magnified.
- Dialogue is possible, but you respond to questions after a short delay (usually two or three seconds).
- If you are asked a question, you opt for the literal meaning (for example: 'Can you tell me your name?' Answer: 'Yes, I can.' You won't say your name unless you are asked directly: 'What is your name?').

One last comment before we get to the heart of the matter: forget everything you've read about hypnosis and its mystic powers. Rest assured that in a state of hypnosis, it is impossible to make you do anything that your subconscious does not wish to do! Obviously, what you can be made to do all depends on the ideas that are stored in the depths of your subconscious.

Hypnosis Can Change Your Life

Today there are a number of very reputable hypnotherapists. You can consult one for a multitude of reasons, and the results will very probably be beneficial. Sound too good to be true?

You must first understand that hypnosis is a means and not an end. It is more of a tool than a treatment as such. It's an open door to your subconscious. For example, under hypnosis you can find out why you have a particular bad habit. And it's only by getting to the source that you can then begin, step by step, to get rid of the undesirable behaviour. On a physical level, hypnosis can alleviate numerous symptoms of disease, and/or prolong periods of remission in incurable disorders. And hypnosis is also worth trying for more minor, though still irksome physical problems. Say you've suffered all your life from stuttering. You will be very surprised when, during a hypnosis session, you are able to speak easily and fluently.

Hypnosis can change your eating habits, make you lose your taste for tobacco, alcohol, coffee and even drugs. It has been used to treat both bulimia and anorexia with remarkable success. If you have depressive tendencies, hypnosis can help you get to the underlying causes of your defeatist attitudes and replace them with a joyous appreciation of life and all it has to offer. Last but not least, hypnosis can replace anaesthesia during surgery, thus avoiding a host of dangerous substances and all the negative side-effects they produce.

How is this possible? Under hypnosis, anaesthesia starts in the brain and not in the affected part of the body. That's what makes all the difference. The extremities receive instructions to desensitize themselves to pain. It's as simple as that. Unfortunately techniques which can replace anaesthesia, such as hypnosis and acupuncture, have not yet been fully accepted by medical authorities in the West.

On a mental level, hypnosis can be used to delve into the very depths of the self, to illuminate weak points, areas where you lack confidence, or the way you inflict wounds on your self-image. Hypnosis can be the key to resuming control of your own life.

One Small Step from Hypnosis to Self-hypnosis

What a hypnotherapist can do for you, you can do for yourself. First of all, you should understand that meditation, explored in Chapter 8, is a form of self-hypnosis. Once you have attained the transcendental state, you will exhibit all the characteristics of a person under hypnosis. So why not use the experience of hypnomeditation to help yourself get what you want out of life?

HAVE YOU HEARD ABOUT AUTO-SUGGESTION?

Hypnosis, whether self-induced or induced by a therapist, operates on the theory of suggestion – the act of impressing messages on the subconscious. There are numerous methods of suggestion and auto-suggestion, hypnosis being one of them. So it follows that the basis of self-hypnosis is auto-suggestion.

To make auto-suggestions, you have to send your subconscious messages that are formulated in a certain way:

- Avoid giving your subconscious orders. As the old saying goes: You don't catch flies with vinegar! In other words, when communicating with your subconscious formulate your messages as a kind of affirmation or authorization ('I can . . .' or 'You can . . .' or 'I am . . .' instead of 'You must . . .').

  It can happen that direct orders are effective ('I must . . .' or 'I want . . .'), but they have to correspond exactly to your situation. It's better to suggest, to support, rather than to use authoritarian language. Trying to order the subconscious around is usually futile, especially for amateurs.

- Be positive. Eliminate negations as much as possible. Avoid impossibilities, refusals, doubts and ambiguities. Get rid of words like 'if', 'maybe' and 'perhaps'. These words may be useful in rounding off the sharp edges of daily communication with our peers, but they don't work on the subconscious. Be affirmative and optimistic. You must be the absolute master of your self!

- Give your subconscious time. When you make auto-suggestions, it's better to give your subconscious the impression that what you want will happen in the near future, instead of instantly. Does that seem strange? Let's look at an example.

  Say you're bothered because you're a few pounds overweight, and you want to use self-hypnosis to slim down. (How to do this will be explained in Chapter 15.) Don't say to your subconscious: 'The extra weight is gone. I have a perfect figure.' Why? Because your subconscious is not completely stupid – it knows perfectly well that you're still overweight. So say instead: 'I will lose some weight every day. I'm getting slimmer and slimmer, and soon I'll get rid of that embarrassing flab completely.'

  Without expressing the slightest doubt, you have allowed yourself the necessary time in which to accomplish your goal – the time your subconscious needs to get to work and trim down your figure.

- Be clear, simple and precise. Avoid clouding your subconscious with a mountain of complicated details. You'll take care of them later. For the moment, keep your suggestions clear.

  It might happen that you feel certain detailed indications are absolutely necessary. The solution in this case is relatively easy: write them down. Read them over before going to sleep. Study them. In this way you will program your conscious mind, and suppress useless information. Do your deep breathing exercises while studying your notes. Relax and concentrate on your message. The subconscious automatically absorbs everything assimilated by the conscious.

WHERE TO START?

You are probably thinking that a certain amount of practice must be necessary. The success of a suggestion-message depends to a large extent not only on what it contains, but on the tone in which it is delivered. Here is a simple method which you can apply to begin your self-hypnosis training. It consists of making auto-suggestions while you sleep. You need three 'tools':

- a tape recorder, with a speaker that can be placed under your pillow
- a tape or cassette

– a bed or comfortable couch where you know you will have no difficulty falling asleep.

THE WORDS TO USE

Here is an example of a message you can tape:

> I am relaxing, I am closing my eyes. I am letting my thoughts flow through my mind without trying to stop them. I am emptying myself. All tension is dissolving from my body and mind.
>
> I cross my hands on my chest. I concentrate all my attention on my hands, on the tips of my fingers. I feel warmth spreading through me. It is a pleasant, beneficial feeling.
>
> My whole body is relaxed, and full of warmth. My muscles are loose. I feel more and more as though I'm floating. I am falling asleep. In a few minutes I will be asleep. But I will continue to hear this message.
>
> My body is totally relaxed, but my mind is alert. When I wake up, I will feel marvellously well. I will be able to accomplish the things I want to do. I will remain healthy in body and mind. I will . . . .
>
> [At this point, repeat the message you wish to send to your subconscious – something like: 'I will rid myself of migraines . . .' or 'I will get my loan . . .' or 'I will pass my exam . . .' and so on. The message should be clear, concise, confident and positive.]
>
> In a few minutes I will wake up. I will feel good. I will feel purified and relaxed.
>
> I will count to three. On the count of three I will wake up, in full control of my faculties, refreshed from my little nap. One . . . two . . . Three. I am awake, I feel great.

COMFORT IS ESSENTIAL

Each night, get comfortable in bed or on a sofa, in a room where you know you won't be disturbed. Limit all external input as much as possible (TV noise, kitchen smells etc.). Choose a room that isn't too 'busy' and over-decorated – a bedroom, for example. Place a fairly thin pillow under your head. Remove any tight clothing. Adjust the temperature of the room if necessary (by closing windows or turning up the heating) so that you aren't cold.

Place the tape recorder near your hand, and the headphones on your pillow (or the speaker under the pillow). Relax completely. Do a few breathing exercises and loosen your muscles. Think about pleasant things, like the people you love or good times in your life. Then press the start button and let the tape roll.

A FEW IMPORTANT NOTES ABOUT THIS METHOD

- The sample message on p. 54 was formulated in the first person. But some of us are in the habit of talking to ourselves in the second person. If you are one of those, don't hesitate to change the message, replacing 'I' with 'you'. Anything that makes suggesting easier is permissible.

- It is obviously better to listen to the message after achieving at least some degree of relaxation. If you are in the habit of doing breathing or visualization exercises, or if you meditate regularly, then you probably won't have any trouble relaxing beforehand. Nevertheless, when you practise auto-suggestion for the first time it's difficult not to feel a little apprehensive and nervous. If you cannot get into the alpha state, stop the exercise and try again the next day. Don't upset yourself by trying too hard – you will only create more problems for yourself.

- You might also be trying the exercise at the wrong time. If you're used to doing physical exercise at night, or if you are used to eating a large meal shortly before going to bed, you might not be able to relax.

- On the other hand, if you're in the habit of taking a nap, or just lying down with a book at a certain time of day, then choose this time to try the exercise. Your body is used to relaxing at that time, and will be easier to manage.

- If you are one of those people for whom music has a calming effect, then why not listen to some for a few minutes before your session?

Surprising as it may seem, some people go to the other extreme to get relaxed and fall into such a deep sleep, that the message on the tape can't wake them up when the exercise is over. Hypnotherapists suggest that this is simply because they don't want to wake up. Sometimes sleep is a refuge, an escape.

Psychotherapists have also had patients fall asleep during a session. This phenomenon is explained by the fact that some patients, having opened doors in the subconscious which they'd rather leave closed, or which scare them, fall asleep to avoid an uncomfortable situation. This is exactly what can happen to you during an auto-suggestion period.

Don't be alarmed if this is true of you, too. You will wake up on your own, when you want to.

Exercises to Change Your Life

Self-hypnosis, like cooking, sports, music and a multitude of other activities, requires practice. The more you practise, the quicker you will attain the state of self-hypnosis and the more effective your suggestions will be. Here is a series of steps which should guide you toward achieving total control of your subconscious through self-hypnosis.

As usual, choose a location where you will not be disturbed. You need about twenty minutes of absolute calm for each session. There are five steps to your practice which, if possible, should be repeated daily.

FIRST STEP: HOW TO MASTER THE MATERIAL WORLD

Light a candle and place it in front of you. Stare at it until your eyelids get heavy. Suggest to yourself that they're getting heavy by repeating, 'My eyelids are heavy . . . I feel them getting heavier . . . I'm looking at the flame . . . My eyelids are getting heavy . . .' and so on, just like a real hypnotist.

After a few moments, close your eyes. Tighten the muscles around your eyes. Become aware of them. Feel them. Concentrate all your attention on the tightened muscles around your eyes. Think about them, visualize them in your mind.

Then say, 'Now I will relax.' And your eye muscles will automatically relax.

You have just taken an important step forward: the victory of mind over matter.

SECOND STEP: THE STAIRCASE

Now relax the rest of your body, as you have learnt to do. Start with the top of your skull, and move right down to your toes. Open your eyes.

Breathe deeply from the abdomen, keeping your gaze fixed on the candle flame. You don't hear anything, you don't feel anything. . . . Your whole being is concentrated on the tiny flame dancing gently before your eyes. . . .

Count from twenty down to one. Imagine you are walking down a staircase, and with each number you take one step down towards the bottom, where there is a black void. This void is a marvellous sleep. You want to dive in – it is pulling you in. From now on, at your own suggestion, you will be able to control your body and mind.

THIRD STEP: THE THERMOSTAT

You suggest that one of your hands is getting cold. . . . It gets colder and colder. . . . It feels as if you are holding it in a bag of ice.

Don't worry if the sensation of cold does not appear right away. The more you practise, the faster you will control your mind. Have patience at the beginning. The most important thing is to believe in what you're doing. The rest will follow. After a few moments, you should feel the tingling which precedes the sensation of cold in your hand.

FOURTH STEP: THE HEAVY FEATHER

Now the time has come to manipulate your hand directly. Tell it that it weighs nothing, that it's floating: 'Left hand [or right], you weigh nothing . . . you're floating in the air . . . you're as light as a feather. . . .' Do this for a few seconds, repeating these phrases.

Once again, if nothing happens don't get discouraged. Do a few breathing exercises, and start again at the beginning of the previous step.

Suggest that your hand and arm rise slowly into the air. With no weight, it rises gently, higher and higher, softly, like a feather. If you feel the muscles in your hand and forearm start to tremble, then you know you're on the right path, even if they don't lift up into the air. Above all, don't doubt your ability. You have already taken a giant step forward. And, of course, if your hand and arm have lifted up – well done!

Relax your muscles. Let your hand and arm resume their original position. Open your eyes. Breathe deeply. Congratulate yourself – you should be proud of what you've accomplished. Welcome to the club of people who are in control of their destiny.

Obviously, the more you practise, the more effective your suggestions will be. After a few sessions, the directions you send your body will become easier and easier to carry out.

WAKING UP

Although we use the term 'sleep' to describe the hypnotic state, don't forget that you can wake yourself up at any time. It is preferable, especially during the first session, to cut yourself off completely from external stimulation, to set up a thick wall between yourself and outside influences. However, even in this state you can still be perfectly conscious of what's going on around you.

On waking, you will experience a feeling of total wellbeing. It's as though you've had a bath in the fountain of youth. So don't wait any longer. Do your first self-hypnosis session today.

CHAPTER 10

Some Advanced Methods for Controlling Your Future

Psychocybernetics

This unfamiliar term is based on a science which, although relatively recent, is becoming more and more important in the study of our cerebral potential. You may know that the term 'cybernetics' refers to theories concerning 'commands', both in living things and in machines. The words 'cybernetic' and 'governor' have the same Greek root.

Psychocybernetics works on the principle that our subconscious is a system possessing a seeking head which is constantly programmed to reach a precise objective. You are the one who chooses the goal, consciously or not. If you program your system for success and happiness, it will be sure to aim for that objective. But in the same way, if you program it for failure, unhappiness and illness, it will strive for those objectives just as ardently.

It has been made clear right from the start of this book that by filling your subconscious with negative thoughts which picture you as incapable, incompetent, physically unattractive, sickly and so on you are sure to experience failure, rejection, depression and physical illness of all kinds. So in order to resolve the problems that are annoying you, and to remain healthy in body and mind, to experience the joy of living, you have to make this system work for you instead of against you.

You have a fantastic machine available to you, subtler and more highly developed than the most sophisticated computer. Learn to use it.

HOW TO GO ABOUT IT

The subconscious is essentially designed to respond to images. It is through these images, consciously created by you, that you can impose your will on the system. The method developed by Dr Maxwell Maltz, author of 'Psycho-Cybernetics', is based on what he calls 'self image', which simply represents our ideal self.

The first step consists of creating a realistic and satisfying self image.

At this stage of your training, you have already developed considerable talents. Even if you haven't perfected the technique of self-hypnosis (what are you waiting for?) you are able to do visualizations, deep breathing, relaxation and perhaps meditation. So you have already gained some mastery over yourself and your subconscious. You should now have no difficulty creating your self image.

RESTORING YOUR SELF IMAGE

1. Look for a few photographs of yourself in your photograph album. We all have some pictures of ourselves that we like. They resemble the ideal person whom we'd like to see in the mirror every morning.

2. Study them carefully. Try to remember all the details: your facial characteristics, your skin texture, your smile, hairstyle, expression.

3. Now retreat to your mental refuge in the usual way.

4. Study your surroundings. Has anything changed since your last visit? Force yourself to register all the sensations evoked by your personal refuge: tactile, visual, auditory and olfactory. Place special emphasis on the colours in your visualization.

5. Now try to relax completely. Do a few breathing exercises.

6. Visualize yourself carrying out some pleasant activity. See yourself as you would like to be, using as a basis the photographic images you studied. Feel the harmony emanating from your being.

Don't stop too quickly. Savour this ideal image of yourself. Tell yourself that this is who you really are, both morally and physically. Everything about you is harmonious and healthy.

Warning

Do you recall the sad story of Narcissus? To punish him for breaking so many hearts a goddess condemned him to fall in love with his own reflection, thus damning him to a slow death of eternal frustration, eaten away by a passion that was impossible to fulfil. . . .

Creating a self image is not an exercise in narcissism. The aim is not to create a self that is unreal, arrogant and haughty. What you're looking for is your real self, healthy and balanced, extracted from the person you really are, and not an illusory phantom.

WHAT CAN YOU DO WITH YOUR IDEAL IMAGE?

In the second part of the exercise you will learn how, by applying the latest discoveries in psychocybernetics, you can get rid of pain, bad habits, migraines, allergies, depression, extra weight and many other common problems. Because when you possess an authentic self image you can use it for multiple ends.

For example, if you want to speed up your recovery after an operation, imagine your ideal self as a robust person, full of get-up-and-go, in the act of doing some healthy exercise or walking in a beautiful forest.

The Three-step Method

This method makes use of techniques which you already know. All you have to do is chain them together, as you will soon see. By using the three-step method you can, among other things:

- Resolve annoying problems
- Regain your energy
- Lose weight and enhance your physical appearance
- Improve your character, become more tolerant and easier to live with
- Get rid of bad habits (tobacco, alcohol, sweets etc.)
- Develop more self-confidence, eliminate fear of speaking in public, excessive shyness etc.

- And, of course, get rid of a multitude of health problems.

First step

Retreat to your mental refuge. Relax completely. Open the knots in your muscles and relax your mind. Look round your refuge. Make a few changes if you like. If you have the time, a few minutes of meditation would be helpful. If not, move on to the next step.

Second step

Do you remember the blackboard technique you studied in Chapter 4? If not, refresh your memory by reading that chapter again.

Suppose the blackboard and the white board and the hammer are still there in your retreat, where you left them. On the blackboard write your problems, your apprehensions, your negative thoughts . . . in short, whatever is bothering you.

If you're looking for the solution to a problem, just leave the problem written out on the blackboard and go to sleep. When you return to your sanctuary the next day, you should find the solution written out on the white board. At that moment define the solution in the form of an image, so that it will be deeply impressed on your subconscious.

If you're working on negative thoughts, don't forget to smash the blackboard with the hammer before writing your positive thoughts on the white board.

Third and last step

This step uses what is called the twenty-one-day method. Here's how it works. Each time you wake up or go to sleep do the following:

1. Put out the light and draw the curtains. Calm yourself. You feel pleasantly sleepy. Now fly to your refuge, breathing deeply and calmly as you have learnt.

2. Write what you want on the white board. Read this message over a number of times, feeling a deep sense of approval each time.

   Let this feeling spread through you. Visualize your new, positive habit, your recovery, the solution to your problem and so on. Try to visualize yourself as if your goal has already been attained.

If you impress your subconscious with positive thoughts, practising the method twice a day, in twenty-one days you should get rid of whatever problem or bad habit is bothering you.

The twenty-one-day technique is most efficient if you avoid visualizing the blackboard once it has served its purpose. Use any means possible to keep it out of your refuge during the whole period. It represents your problems, your bad habits, pains and everything negative about your life. After retreating to your personal refuge, go to sleep each night with the white board in front of you, inscribed with your positive thoughts. Remember that if you interrupt your practice for only one day, you'll have to start all over again.

Last, you can only use this method to resolve one problem at a time. For example, don't try to stop drinking and stop getting upset in traffic jams, and do more exercise and be more polite to your neighbour, all at the same time. During the twenty-one-day period, your subconscious concentrates on only one of your desires. It is incapable of dealing with diverse problems at the same time, and all its efforts are directed towards achieving one goal.

If you aren't satisfied with the results you obtain from the twenty-one-day method, persevere in this way:

1. Apply the twenty-one-day method.

2. Let a week pass during which you don't think about your problem at all. Your subconscious will use this time to come up with a solution.

3. Start another twenty-one-day cycle.

4. When it's over, interrupt the process for another week.

Keep doing this for three months. Be confident!

Sophronization

The word 'sophronization' is derived from 'sophrology' which, in etymological terms means the science or methodology for attaining serenity. Today, sophrology is defined as the study of all states of consciousness, whatever methods are used to induce them. Therefore it includes hypnosis, meditation, certain extrasensory phenomena and numerous other methods.

Sophronization consists of a series of methods designed to induce an intermediary state between sleep and waking, during which the subconscious is open to communication. Does this sound exactly like a definition of hypnosis?

Specialists in the field affirm that the main difference between sophronization and hypnosis is not in the quality of the induced state, but in the nature of the relationship between the sophronist and his or her subject. A hypnotherapist, using willpower, can incite you to relax and fall asleep. A sophronist only guides the subject, without imposing his will. The subject participates actively in the induction of the sophronic state. His or her will is not replaced by that of the therapist.

There are multiple methods of sophronization, and anyone can create their own technique. The especially original method described here is called dynamic relaxation. It was developed and perfected by Dr Caycedo when he was Professor of Psychiatry at Barcelona University, and has numerous applications. It can be used to combat a wide range of allergies, and to get rid of bad habits. It can improve self-confidence and eliminate stagefright, nausea, exaggerated shyness and the infamous inferiority complex.

DYNAMIC RELAXATION

How can relaxation be dynamic? Surely this concept is a contradiction in terms?

Dr Caycedo had the ingenious idea of combining mental exercises of oriental origin with occidental methods of sophronization. The result is a technique that links movement to relaxation. His goal is to create harmony between body and mind, a quality which is so lacking in modern Western society.

Theoretically, dynamic relaxation is done in a group. As far as you are concerned, you can apply the method in either of two ways.

TO COMBAT HAYFEVER

At this stage you should have had at least some practice with self-hypnosis. Sophronization is an advanced method, so it is essential for you to have passed through the basic stages. You should already be in the habit of taping messages and listening to them each night before you go to sleep. For this new exercise, you go from messages to images.

While recording your message, and when you come to the part that contains your suggestions ('I will pass my exam . . .' etc.) replace the verbal message with an image. Here's an example.

You want to get rid of your hayfever. As you are taping your message close your eyes and visualize yourself walking in the country in May or June, when the pollen season is at its height. Describe your surroundings out loud. Feel the hot sun on your back. Listen to the birds chirping in the trees. Now breathe slowly and deeply. Describe how you feel as the air enters your nostrils. Your sinuses are perfectly healthy. Your head is perfectly clear. Your eyes are dry. Speak into the mike, describing these sensations while you visualize yourself walking in the sunny countryside, despite the fact that the air is full of pollen.

Once the image is taped, open your eyes slowly and end the recording in the usual way. Listen to the tape as you would usually do.

The following spring, if you are confident and haven't let any doubts propagate in your mind, you won't need to go to the chemist's to equip yourself with all kinds of antihistamines.

SWISS SKIERS' EXERCISE

This exercise comes from a programme that was mainly developed for the Swiss Olympic ski team in the sixties. After the skiers had completed the programme, their performances were considerably improved. They acquired more self-confidence, learned to concentrate and control themselves, and got the most out of their physical conditioning and the advice of their trainers. What works for an Olympic team can't be bad for us ordinary mortals.

1. Relax little by little. Empty your mind. You don't have to reach the transcendental state, but really clear your mind and isolate yourself from the exterior world.
2. Now rotate your head slowly, first from left to right and then in the opposite direction (six rotations to each side). You might want to imagine that you're holding a flashlight in your teeth, with which you are tracing circles of light.
3. Contract your neck muscles by tensing your face (fifteen times). Don't look in a mirror – you might think you're another Frankenstein's monster!
4. Breathe rapidly from the abdomen as you have learnt to do, until your lower back starts to hurt.
5. Breathe out through your mouth. Make sure to empty your lungs and stomach of air. Hold your breath a moment before breathing in again, using the rhythm you have already practised (8–4–8– see p. 35).
6. Breathe out all your air through the nose. Hold your breath.

7. Breathe in deeply through your mouth. Hold your breath. Breathe out through your nose. Repeat this exercise three to five times.
8. While continuing your deep breathing, rotate each arm separately, and then do both together.
9. Do some more deep breathing using the 8–4–8 rhythm.
10. Contract all your muscles, one by one.
11. Continue the 8–4–8 breathing.
12. Breathe out and at the same time curve your spine. Breathe in and at the same time straighten your spine out, drawing a circle with your upper body. Hold your breath for three full circles, then breathe out.
13. Stand up slowly.
14. Finish the session as you normally would.

The Simonton Method

The method developed by Drs Carl and Stephanie Simonton, cancer specialist and psychologist respectively, is primarily designed for people suffering from serious diseases. This method will be referred to again later in the book, in Chapter 17 which deals with these kinds of diseases.

But everyone, healthy or ill, is recommended to follow this very complete programme which begins with learning how to relax and ends with acquiring certain skills which will improve your daily life.

First, here is the relaxation exercise recommended by the Simontons to all patients suffering from serious illness, but which can benefit you as well.

PROGRESSIVE RELAXATION EXERCISE

You might want to record the following instructions on cassette, so that you can listen to them when doing the exercise. Or you can ask someone to read them out loud to you, if you prefer. This exercise should last about fifteen minutes, and be done two or three times a day. You will see your state of relaxation grow deeper as time goes on.

1. Make yourself comfortable in a room with the lights dimmed. Place your feet flat on the ground and close your eyes.
2. Breathe deeply and try to become conscious of your breathing rhythm.

3. With each breath out, repeat the word 'Relax'.

4. Feel the tension in your face. Create an image for this tension, for example a string pulled tight in a knot, or an elastic band stretched tight, or a closed fist.

5. Now feel your face relax. A wave of relaxation surges through your whole body.

6. Close your eyes and contract all your facial muscles. Then release them, feeling your whole body relax.

7. Repeat the procedure with each part of your body, from top to bottom: the neck, shoulders, arms, chest, abdomen, thighs, calves, ankles, feet and toes. Take your time. First visualize the tension and release. Then contract the muscles before relaxing them.

8. When every part of your body is relaxed, stay quiet for a moment, with your mind empty.

9. Now feel your eyelids growing lighter as you become conscious of your surroundings.

10. Slowly open your eyes.

As you see, this exercise makes use of visualization as well as relaxation techniques. For the tension to disappear, you have to imagine it in concrete form. The Simonton Method is essentially based on the concrete visualization of harmful elements, whatever they may be – from muscle tension to pathogenic elements.

DEFINE YOUR PHILOSOPHY OF LIFE

The programme consists of principles concerning everyday life, the most important of which are outlined here. These principles are also incorporated in Chapter 17.

Once again, you don't have to be ill to adopt the Simonton philosophy. The best medicine is prevention and here is a way to apply that bit of wisdom.

- *Accept your body.* Any unpleasant symptom, whether it's just a rash from an insect bite, or the ravages of one of the many forms of cancer, tends to create resentment in ourselves towards our own body. To get better, or to stay healthy, you must love your body and be on good terms with it. It's not your body which is to blame, it's your mind. Ally yourself with your body to fight or prevent disease.

- *Make plans.* This doesn't mean living for the future, but rather living in the present while imagining the future. If you set accessible goals and have fun achieving them, then you are making an active statement negating death and affirming a pleasant future.

- *Get rid of hate and resentment.* Don't let destructive feelings wear you down. Your immunity or recovery depends, to a large extent, on the way you perceive the world and the people who inhabit it. Love, and take pleasure in being loved. Look for the positive side in others. Only rarely will you fail to find one.

- *Communicate with the people around you.* Spend some time getting to know your family better, your friends, your colleagues etc. Be tolerant of their lifestyles. Create an aura of benevolence around you. Open the doors to communication: speak, ask questions and listen.

The Roger Vittoz Method

Dr Vittoz (1863–1904), a doctor who was confronted with the psychosomatic problems of some of his patients, designed a method which rapidly spread beyond the borders of his native Switzerland. He called his programme 'cerebral control re-education', and he described cerebral control as 'an inherent faculty . . . meant to balance the unconscious brain'.

So his method is principally a technique for mastering the subconscious. When 'cerebral control' is deficient, we fall prey to uncertainty, doubt, anxiety, fear – in short all the destructive influences which can sprout and grow in the fertile ground of the subconscious.

Dr Vittoz originally developed the method to treat psychopaths. Little by little, because of increasing demonstrations of its effectiveness, it was adopted by other doctors and therapists and applied to patients suffering from a variety of physical and psychosomatic ailments. The Vittoz Method is divided into three basic elements:

- re-establishment of cerebral control
- perfecting cerebral control
- maintaining cerebral balance.

RE-ESTABLISHMENT OF CEREBRAL CONTROL

Two main exercises are used to achieve this first step. Their objective is to concentrate on sensations throughout the body, in order to emphasize the emitting and receiving capacity of the brain.

Exercise to become conscious of your corporeal self

First step
1. Get comfortable on your bed or on a sofa. Dim the lights.
2. Start to become aware of your body. Try to 'feel' your limbs, your head etc.
3. Now try to become aware of your surroundings: noises, colours, smells, the feel of the material on which you're lying, the quality of the air and so on.

This first step helps you become conscious of your 'corporeal self'. It is essential if you want to get rid of anxiety, doubts and lack of self-confidence.

Second step
4. Now relax completely, as you have learnt to do. It doesn't matter which method you use, as long as it works.

Third step
5. Stop thinking and associating ideas in your mind. Let your brain 'feel'. Become conscious of all the parts of your body, one after the other.

Here's a trick to make this easier: you can imagine that you are rubbing each part of your body, in order to 'feel' it with your conscious mind. Visualize yourself doing the action.

When the exercise is finished, remain quiet for a few minutes before getting up.

The old clock exercise

In this exercise you will use mental images rather than the tactile sensations used in the previous exercise.

1. Get comfortable on your sofa and relax, using your preferred technique.
2. Retreat to your mental refuge.

3. There you will visualize a clock, an old grandfather clock, made of smooth, well-polished wood with ornate hands. Through an oblong window you see the pendulum swinging.
4. The pendulum is made of brass. Its arm and base shine. The base is a disc divided into two parts, one matt, the other shiny.
5. The pendulum swings back and forth regularly. Watch it – back and forth, back and forth.
6. If you're a musician, you might want to replace the clock with a metronome. Use the same procedure.
7. After a few minutes, return from your mental refuge and open your eyes.

PERFECTING CEREBRAL CONTROL

Up to now, almost all the techniques discussed were designed to put you in touch with your subconscious. However, this part of the Vittoz method aims to improve our mastery of conscious actions, after teaching us to master our physical sensations by doing the exercises described above. According to Dr Vittoz, it is when the mind wanders and actions become automatic that doubts, anxieties and insecurities develop in us.

Starting with actions, lack of control spreads to the mind, which then becomes more and more negative. So here are two very simple exercises which are surprisingly effective in combating this tendency.

Exercise to dispel fatigue

This exercise consists simply of taking a walk and consciously feeling the sensations you encounter.

Each time your foot touches the ground, feel the ground under you. Make sure each step is accompanied by an easy movement of the arms. Experience the feeling in your whole body. All your senses should be involved: not only touch but sight, sound, taste and smell. These sensations should occupy your whole consciousness.

When you get home from work, do the exercise by walking round a room a few times, or by going up and down a flight of stairs. An extraordinarily pleasant feeling will take hold of you. Being totally conscious of your actions will dissipate the fatigue you have accumulated during the day.

Exercise to develop concentration

This exercise is as simple as the preceding one. You are going to read out loud. But be careful – you must not let your mind wander at any time during the exercise. This is harder than it sounds, since we all have the tendency to daydream.

The aim of the exercise is the same as the last one. So while you read, try to be perfectly conscious of every word, and of the sound of your voice. If your mind starts to wander, if one idea leads to a series of other thoughts, then stop, go back and read the passage over again.

But it's not that difficult – it's rare to lose track completely when reading out loud.

Follow this procedure:

1. First read the passage silently to yourself.
2. Then read it again out loud. You will notice the difference between the two readings. The first lends itself to distraction, while the second tends to limit it.
3. Go back to the beginning and read out loud again, trying to be conscious of every sensation: the book itself, the smell of the paper, your own voice, the words, the punctuation, the consonants, the rhythm of your reading.
4. Close the book and force yourself to repeat what you've just read. There's a trick that may help you: imagine that there's an attentive listener sitting in front of you.

This exercise, while very simple, is extremely effective.

MAINTAINING CEREBRAL BALANCE

Once you have recovered your cerebral control and learnt to develop it, you just have to keep it in balance so as not to lose it again. This balance is achieved by eliminating pathogenic thoughts. You must make these thoughts of doubt disappear, and forget any destructive ideas. This is the only way you can keep your cerebral balance intact.

Dr Vittoz's technique makes use of a few exercises which are progressively more difficult. They all depend on the mental image of erasing, of disappearing. The few ideas presented here are not at all exhaustive – have fun finding your own exercise subjects.

Exercise for forgetting and erasing

Numbers

1. Get comfortable in your mental refuge.
2. In your mind, write down a few numbers on a piece of paper.
3. Still in your mind, pick up an eraser and rub out all the numbers, one after the other.
4. Repeat this exercise a few times.

Letters

5. Now write down some letters on your sheet of paper.
6. Pick up your eraser and rub them out.
7. Repeat the exercise a few times.

Words

8. This time write down whole sentences, thoughts that bother you or embarrass you, memories that are eating away at you, and so on.
9. Once more, rub them all out with your eraser.
10. Repeat the exercise a few times.

When you get used to doing this exercise, the first two steps can be left out. Just do the part using words.

Although very simple, these exercises are extremely effective in getting rid of pathogenic thoughts. There are many people who, thanks to Dr Vittoz's programme, have regained their taste for life, their health, appetite, ability to sleep and self-confidence.

Coué's Universal Method

When the French pharmacist Emile Coué set up his auto-suggestion clinic at the turn of the century, he had no idea that in a few years it would make him world-famous. Coué developed the therapeutic power of auto-suggestion. According to him, we all possess the psychic potential which should enable us to cure most of the disorders we suffer from, and to overcome the problems we encounter in life. He believed that we depend far too much on medication and other types of external treatments, and not enough on the spontaneous healing abilities that we all possess. So his method consists mainly of 'awakening' these self-healing powers.

The fact that we have them is undeniable. You just have to read the conclusions of recent studies on the effects of placebos to be convinced.

THE PLACEBO EFFECT

Eighty-three patients suffering from arthritis were given pills containing nothing but sugar instead of their regular medication, aspirin or cortisone. A second group received its usual medication. The percentage of patients who reported experiencing relief was the same among patients who received the panacea as among those who got their usual medication.

In addition, when an injection of sterilized water was given to those who had been given a panacea, but who did not report any relief, 64 per cent of them then said they felt relief of their symptoms (apparently injections have a stronger impact than pills on the patient's expectations, and have nothing to do with the medical value of the different treatments).

Carl Simonton, *Getting Well Again*

A placebo (from the Latin 'I will please') is a totally benign substance that is given to a patient while he or she believes that the substance is an active medication.

Studies on the subject have shown that in 35–45 per cent of cases (and sometimes more) the placebo produces the same curative effect as the medication. This is especially true of placebos which replace analgesics, laxatives, tranquillizers, antacids and antihistamines. They have even been used with some success on patients suffering from certain types of cancer.

Our willpower can have the same effect on our organism and its weaknesses as a placebo. And that's what the Coué method is all about.

THE FORMULA THAT CURES

Coué's programme incorporates an important element: relaxation. So if you decide to try this programme, don't forget to practise your relaxation exercises.

Coué's method may sound simplistic, but it has worked for lots of people.

Here are the main steps:

1. Towards the end of each day, stretch out for a few minutes in your mental refuge.
2. Relax, using whichever method you prefer. Coué suggested using a technique which has since become famous under the name of 'progressive relaxation'.
3. Get rid of all your negative ideas and unpleasant thoughts. For example, think of your mind as the ocean, very early on a summer morning. The surface is smooth and calm, without a ripple.
4. Then repeat this sentence at least twenty times: 'Every day, in all things, I am becoming better and better.'
5. Repeat the sentence in a calm monotone.
6. Next move on to another essential idea: 'I am happy and strong. I am myself.' Repeat this a dozen times.
7. Go back to the first sentence and repeat it a dozen times.

HOW TO FORMULATE YOUR IDEAS CORRECTLY

Don't drown your subconscious with wishes. Be satisfied with a single, detailed idea. Your subconscious cannot diversify. You have to let it concentrate all its efforts on one problem at a time. Save other problems for later.

Formulate your wish as if it were already accomplished
The subconscious must understand the desired result as something already acquired. So don't say things like. 'I would really like to . . .' or 'I would prefer . . .'. Instead say, 'I am . . .' or 'I have . . .' Eliminate the distant future (think in terms of the near future) and especially the conditional from your vocabulary when impressing your subconscious with your desires.

Avoid bringing your willpower into play
If you try to impose your will, you risk producing the opposite result. So don't say, 'I want . . .' or even worse 'I would like . . .' Your subconscious will probably resist.

Avoid negations and ideas with negative connotations
Don't say, 'I will not catch cold' or 'My heart is not sick.' Rather, formulate the idea as an affirmation: 'I am in perfect health . . .' or 'My heart is fine.'

Use the clearest and simplest formulations possible

You are not going to be marked for rhetoric or eloquence. Forget about complex sentences that tend to run on and on. Get right to the point, without any embellishment. And avoid ambiguity.

Write your formulations down before each session

Then memorize them. This practical habit will save you a lot of confusion.

PART TWO

DAY-TO-DAY PRACTICE

Progress in medicine will not result from building bigger and better equipped hospitals, or more pharmaceutical factories. It will depend on imagination, on observing sick people and then meditating about what is observed and finally experimenting in the calm of the laboratory, to discover the mysteries of the human mind, which lie hidden behind the veil of chemical structures.

Dr Alexis Carrell, *Unknown Man*

CHAPTER 11

How to Activate Your Body's Natural Defences

A Rule for Living: Optimism

Here, in a few words, is a rule that you should make your philosophy of life: brighten all your words and thoughts with the light of optimism. Let's start with a little test. Just choose the response, A or B, which corresponds to your spontaneous reaction – but be honest.

- Place in front of you a glass which contains water, wine, or juice or anything else you like to drink. The glass is only half filled. Your first thought is:
  A – This glass is half empty.
  B – This glass is half full.

- You pass a superb house just like the house of your dreams. Your first thought is:
  A – I'll never have the means to buy a house like that.
  B – I hope the people living in that house know how lucky they are.

- You find out that someone on your staff is going to be promoted, but you don't know who. Your first thought is:
  A – Well, anyway, it won't be me.
  B – There's a chance it might be me.

- As you leave for work, you notice that the sky is overcast:
  A – You get a raincoat and umbrella, just in case.
  B – You tell yourself that the sky will clear up during the day.

- You're going to pick someone up at the station. The train arrives, but your friend isn't on it. You think:

  A – He (or she) had an accident on the way.

  B – He (or she) missed the train. I'll call home to see if there's a message, and I'll wait for the next train.

ARE YOU ALREADY EQUIPPED?

If your answer to three, four or five of these questions was A, it's time you took stock of your mental situation! Your life is probably in complete disarray. You have no means of defence against the attacks of disease. You are the ideal prey for all kinds of infections, stress, depression and serious illnesses like cancer. Your immune system probably has the same defeatist attitude as you do.

If you only responded to one or two questions with an A, then you're on the right track but you still have some work to do. And of course if you answered B to all the questions, then you have nothing to learn on the subject of optimism. You are well equipped to fight disease. You're probably seldom sick or depressed. You belong to that group of people about whom others say, 'Oh, he [or she] never has any problems. His health is amazing. And he's successful at everything he does.' Don't change! You possess one of the keys to health and happiness.

But what if you belong to one of the first two categories? You have to learn to be optimistic again. Pessimistic thoughts are destructive once they become established in the subconscious. They eat away at your psychological and physiological defences, and poison you in every sense of the word.

You've probably read newspaper or magazine articles which state that the percentage of people who get cancer is significantly higher among divorced or separated couples. This is a concrete example of how negative thinking, pessimism and depression can ravage our system. But all is not lost. Take courage, and start working on seeing the bright side of things. The effort is worth it.

Here is an exercise which will help you observe your own thoughts and words.

HOW TO ELIMINATE YOUR NEGATIVE THOUGHTS

Carry a pen and a small notebook with you wherever you go. For two weeks, write down every negative or pessimistic thought you have, along with the date. For example:

- I'm going to fail my exam.
- If there are any budget cuts, I'll lose my job.
- With this filthy weather, I'm sure to catch cold.
- When you really need to keep warm, there's always a power cut.
- I'm going to ruin this pie crust just because I've got friends coming for dinner.

After about a week you'll probably be writing down a lot more negative thoughts – not because you're thinking more of them but because you've gradually become used to noticing them instead of letting them slip by.

Then for the next two weeks do the opposite: write down your positive thoughts and date them.

At the end of the four week period, sit down with your notebook. Count the negative thoughts, and then the positive thoughts. Theoretically, if you have work to do on your state of mind you should have more negative thoughts than positive ones.

Now look at each of your negative thoughts and imagine that you're replacing each one with a positive thought. For example, if you wrote: 'What a drag, it's raining again and I can't play tennis . . .' replace it with something like: 'Well, it's raining. I can try out my new raincoat . . .' or 'Since it's raining, I can use the time to clear out my shelves . . .'.

Repeat the exercise the following week. If you've been honest with yourself, and if you've really made an effort to count your thoughts, the gap between the numbers of negative and positive thoughts should have diminished. Eventually, you'll discover that your negative thoughts have all but disappeared. You'll have learnt to see the bright side of things, which is no small accomplishment in itself.

Get Rid of Fatigue

Have you ever noticed, while browsing in a library or bookshop, how many titles contain the word 'fatigue' or 'tired'? Fatigue is one of the curses of the twentieth century, along with stress, insomnia, headaches and/or backache, all of which will be discussed later. We are all subject to fatigue.

But we're not talking about physical fatigue, which is healthy and beneficial – like the fatigue we feel after a day spent outdoors, or after strenuous exercise or a good spring clean, or after two hours at the piano. No. The fatigue that we're talking about is more a kind of endless lassitude, a deep feeling of discouragement whose source is certainly not a dose of healthy physical effort. Added to the mental or physical fatigue of a long day in the workplace, we often find a sense of boredom and disgust with the work itself. And that's not all.

When we get home, we have to deal with all kinds of chores like cooking, feeding (both physically and psychologically) the family, cleaning the house, washing the dishes, getting ready for the next day, making phone calls, taking care of bills, writing letters and so on. This kind of lifestyle seems almost purposefully designed to create negative fatigue.

FINDING THE ENERGY AND ENTHUSIASM YOU NEED

Here's some good news: we can all reduce negative fatigue, if not eliminate it completely.

You probably know people who are always full of energy, always enthusiastic. For them, each new day is full of promise. They jump out of bed, sing in the shower, take immense pleasure in a delicious and nourishing breakfast, and then face the day with delight, seeming to glide through it on a cloud.

How do they manage it? The first thing, obviously, is to lead a sensible life, free of bad habits (tobacco, alcohol, sweets, coffee, animal fat, too much meat etc.) which burn up our store of energy. Make exercise (cycling, walking, yoga, swimming, tennis etc.) a priority. Actually, our store of energy works like a well: the more we use, the more we produce.

Another cause of fatigue, in no way negligible, is depression which results from working. Did you know that in the Western world 70 per cent of the population do not like their work? However, we still spend a minimum of seven to eight hours a day working, which means a third of the entire day.

So if you want to combat fatigue, try to find work that you enjoy doing. And then what? Then, train your mind to rid itself of fatigue. Most of the techniques of relaxation, respiration and meditation that you have encountered in this book are also excellent for getting rid of fatigue.

THE BENEFITS OF BREATHING

For whatever kind of effort you want to make, whether intellectual or physical, the most effective method of channelling energy is through rhythmic breathing. It consists mainly of adapting your respiratory rhythm to your cardiac rhythm. In the beginning, adopt an 8–4–8 rhythm (breathe in for eight heartbeats). If you want to make the most of your psychic and physical energy, you should practise this exercise regularly in the quiet of your personal retreat.

It might happen that you want to enrich your store of energy for a precise purpose – an exam, for instance, or a sporting event. If so, concentrate your breathing on the parts of the body that you will be needing most (brain for an exam, limbs for a race). If you've forgotten the technique, turn to Chapter 6 and reread the section on breathing.

EXERCISE TO OVERCOME FATIGUE

Here are some exercises which are especially effective for recharging your system with psychic and physical energy. They won't take up much of your time. But, as usual, you should do them regularly.

1. Get comfortable in your mental sanctuary.
2. Relax, breathing deeply.
3. Once you are well installed in your oasis of peace and serenity, start using your powers of visualization.

Telephone image
4. Visualize a telephone that's ringing, that keeps on ringing and doesn't stop ringing. If you find it amusing, you can even imagine the phone jumping up and down as if in a cartoon film.
5. Now imagine yourself sitting comfortably next to the ringing telephone. You can visualize yourself reading a good book, for example, or sitting at your desk drawing (if you like drawing) or looking through a photograph album. In other words, the image of the telephone which is bothering you with its ring must be linked to an image of yourself in the act of doing something you enjoy and that relaxes you.

Performance image
6. Still comfortable in your mental retreat, imagine yourself doing one of the exercises you like. Let's say you enjoy cycling.
7. You are riding through the beautiful countryside on your state-of-the-art mountain bike. You can feel the warm tarmacadam under your tyres, you hear birds singing, crickets chirping, the far-off sound of sheep. You feel the heat of the sun on your back, and your eyes feast on the myriad colours of the countryside.

8. After a few minutes, you arrive home, still cycling.

Many people have stated that this exercise is effective not only for getting rid of fatigue built up over a day's work, but also for enhancing their sports performance. So it's a real bargain! Of course, if you don't like cycling you can visualize another sport: tennis, hiking, sailing, skiing . . . the possibilities are infinite.

EXERCISE TO RECHARGE YOUR BATTERIES

This exercise, as its names implies, is designed to recharge your batteries when you feel run down. If you have the time to do both this exercise and the previous one, then you will have a complete anti-fatigue programme: after first regaining your calm, you recharge your store of energy.

1. Get comfortable on a couch and relax.
2. Now imagine that you're walking in a dense wood. The trees reach majestically towards the sky. The sun can hardly penetrate the foliage to cast its light on the path on which you're walking. You are in a corridor of living green. You walk calmly, feeling a thick layer of dried leaves underfoot. You breathe in deeply, filling your lungs with the fresh scent of pine. You listen to the birds singing, and the squirrels and other small creatures rustling in the under-growth, foraging for food. You feel fine.
3. After walking through the wood for a few minutes you see a bright light in the distance. You move closer, until you make out a clearing with a little brook of pure babbling water.
4. You stand beside the brook. You sit down. The ground is soft and dry. The brook water is crystal-clear. You lean over it.
5. The bed of the stream is covered with multi-coloured stones. You look at them, as the sun reflects off them. Multi-coloured rays shine back at you. You feel their energy enveloping you. You stay like that for a few moments.
6. Now open your eyes. You are refreshed, recharged and ready to take on the world!

Stress: A Devouring Dragon

It's obvious that not all kinds of stress are harmful. For example, although tiring, the stress resulting from getting ready for a pleasant event is not likely to weaken our defences. On the contrary, it fills you with enthusiasm and ardour, makes you optimistic and energetic. At such times, we are practically invulnerable, because we feel invulnerable. On the other hand stress that depletes our energy, that results in feelings of discouragement, lassitude, depression and a whole range of physical disorders, must be eliminated.

Easier said than done, you say. How can we eliminate stress each day of our lives? Although it may be impossible to change the world, we can change the way we react to it.

THE CAUSE OF TROUBLE

Why do we allow ourselves to be devoured by stress? Psychologists have discovered hundreds of factors which contribute to stress, but don't be discouraged by this. It is probable that the stress you experience is caused by one or a few of the following reasons, which are really very straightforward:

- You have inherited a tendency to succumb to stress (observe your parents' behaviour when faced with stress).
- You are afraid, and are drowning yourself with thoughts of 'I should' (I should not make mistakes, I should be happy, I should show more affection to such and such a person, I should learn to cook better, I should be more pleasant etc.).
- Your character generates stress if you are over-competitive, perfectionist or always in a hurry.
- You suppress normal, essential feelings like anger and sadness for a variety of reasons (upbringing, fear of rejection etc.).
- You have bad eating habits. You absorb too much sugar, caffeine or alcohol, while forgetting about certain essential vitamins and minerals. You suffer from a vitamin deficiency.
- You suffer from certain chronic pains.
- If you're a woman, you suffer from PMT (pre-menstrual tension) and all its unpleasant effects (mood changes, breast soreness, water retention, migraines and so on).

HOW TO GET RID OF STRESS

You can easily remedy certain stress factors first by changing your lifestyle, and by applying some of the excellent dietary advice that can be found in the numerous books on nutrition available in bookshops.

The second way to tackle stress consists of recharging your energy batteries on a regular basis, as you have just learnt to do in the section on fatigue. When we are full of energy, the effects of stress on the system are greatly diminished.

The third method consists of practising anti-stress exercises which will allow you once and for all to get rid of the stress that is eating away at your life. The best of these is the three-step anti-stress programme.

The programme consists of three stages, the second of which is a form of inductive hypnosis. It would therefore be wise to tape the entire exercise. Once a day you should get comfortable on your bed or a sofa and play it back.

First step: descending

1. Relax. Breathe deeply a number of times. Relax completely and try to empty your mind of thoughts.
2. You hear the sounds around you, but you place no importance on them. A wall grows between you and any disturbing sounds. Enclose yourself in your own silence.
3. You find yourself at the top of a stairway. You can make out the first few steps, but further down all you see is darkness.
4. You start walking down slowly. Gradually, as the darkness becomes more enveloping, a feeling of wellbeing surrounds you. Sleep spreads over you like a velvet cover. You are marvellously relaxed. You feel light and you feel good.
5. No tension can reach you now. You are completely protected from any kind of stress. Other people may be agitated, but you are not one of them. You function at your own speed, following your own internal rhythm, and everything is in harmony.

Second step: stress is conquered

1. Let your hidden feelings rise to the surface. Study them, and sort them out. Keep the ones that please you, and reject the rest. It's normal to feel depressed sometimes. But you then have to free yourself of this melancholy feeling. Don't let it poison you. You are free because you're able to reject feelings that make you sad or that depress you.
2. You are a completely independent being, with your personal joy and sadness. You are healthy and good. Each time you feel tension growing in you, you find protection behind your shield. You feel

protected night and day. You can almost see the tension crashing against your shield, unable to pierce it.

3. Your days pass harmoniously, at the rhythm you choose. You are satisfied with your accomplishments and with your life in general. You are affectionate towards the people close to you, and are appreciated in turn by those around you. Your actions are positive.

4. At this point, form a positive reaction to some event that is important to you; for example, if you know you can't meet a deadline, tell yourself that you won't let it become an obsession – that you've done your best and that you're satisfied with your efforts.

5. You are happy, because your new attitude makes your life even more pleasant and serene. You are free of stress!

Third step: ascending

1. Enjoy the feeling of wellbeing that pervades you for a few moments more. Then start climbing back up the stairway, counting from one to ten.

2. Say farewell to stress and welcome to a life of freedom and happiness.

Illness – What's that?

Of course we would all love to eliminate the word 'ill' from our vocabulary. How many times have you poured out your troubles to someone, only to have that person take you aside and exclaim, 'But you're in great health! That's the most important thing.'

But what is health? Being in good health means, first of all, being free of physical and mental illnesses. But health also means living a harmonious and balanced life, feeling that you belong in the universe. It means taking pleasure in the little things in nature, like a drop of dew on a flower, or the shiny coat of an animal, the smile of a child or the smell of fresh-cut grass. All these are also part of being healthy.

Illness is a signal which our body sends out. It lets us know, through physical symptoms, that our natural harmony is disturbed, that we're somehow out of balance. To remain healthy, and banish the word 'illness' from our vocabulary as much as possible, we must avoid anything that disturbs our inner balance.

THE BEST FOUNDATIONS FOR LASTING HEALTH

1. Avoid poisoning your mind with negative, pessimistic or unpleasant thoughts. Read the first part of this chapter over again. Practise the self-analysis exercise regularly.

2. Force yourself to be truthful. Telling lies has a disastrous effect on the immune system. They create stress, which can be measured physically using the well-known lie detector apparatus. Even if it seems difficult sometimes, be frank and honest – but without, of course, being brutal or cruel.

3. Be tolerant. Look at the people around you with a benevolent attitude. Don't condemn them, or criticize them too quickly. Never be spiteful, cynical or uncaring.

4. Help other people. Don't forget that our negative actions always return to haunt us, and vice versa. You will harvest the benefits of all positive actions in the form of good health and wellbeing.

5. Each day spend a few moments in your mental retreat, your secret sanctuary. Take pleasure in the feeling of wellbeing that this place produces in you.

6. Recharge your store of psychic energy as often as possible, using the 'luminous sphere' exercise (see p. 30).

7. Sleep as long as your body requires – it's our greatest reward after a tiring day. Don't deprive yourself of your resting hours on the pretext of having too many things to do: the price you'll pay will be out of all proportion to the advantages you may gain.

8. Laugh and cry. Laughter releases hormonal processes that stimulate the immune system. If you've lost the ability to laugh and your sense of humour, try to get it back by reading amusing books or watching funny movies or plays. A good dose of laughter every day will keep you healthy.

9. And finally, two pillars of health: a balanced diet and regular exercise.

Don't Allow Yourself to Grow Old

Life expectancy is increasing from year to year, notably as a result of the improvement in our living conditions. In general we live at least half our lives after the age of forty, which in earlier centuries was considered old.

Therefore, if we want to take full advantage of the years which are before us once the burden of financial pressures has been relieved, and the task of raising a family has been accomplished, we have to learn to contain the ageing process.

How can we prevent ourselves from ageing? Obviously, some factors are out of our control, starting with heredity. But others could, and should, be modified. The fight against physiological ageing begins, as you've probably guessed, with the application of the principles for leading a sensible, healthy life as described earlier. From the psychological point of view there's one principle – well-worn but true – which you should always remember: you're only as old as you feel. If you feel young, you'll stay young. If you feel old, you cannot escape ageing.

But what can you do so that you always feel young? The answer is very simple: you just have to find the fountain of youth.

THE FOUNTAIN OF YOUTH

If this sounds like an idea from a fairytale or mythology, never mind that. It's an idea that works, so don't be prejudiced about trying it out. Do the following exercise faithfully for three months.

1. Every day, for example before you go to sleep, when you are relaxed and happy to be back in your comfortable nest, close your eyes and go to your mental retreat.
2. Once there, visualize your personal fountain of youth. Anything is possible – it's just a question of imagination. You may want your fountain to look like a mountain waterfall, wild and free, cold and crystal-clear as it thunders down between majestic pine trees; or you may prefer a volcanic lake, deep and mysterious, of an incredible turquoise blue. You might prefer a thermal hot spring, channelled through a magnificent marble fountain, carved with sculptures of mythological gods, or maybe just a simple stone trough, like the ones in old village squares.
3. When you have finalized your fountain of youth, remove your clothes and dive in. Then imagine that you emerge healthy and young, free of all the little aches and pains which, although not serious, make life hard to appreciate.
4. Imagine that your hair and skin are shining in the sun, covered with

millions of droplets of rejuvenating, cleansing water. Look closely at yourself. You see yourself as you were at twenty. You don't have any more wrinkles, any more grey hair. Your back is straight, your legs firm and strong. Your skin is soft and smooth, and your cheeks are full of colour. Feel the energy entering all your pores.

5. Now dive into your fountain of youth again. Repeat the process a few times. Let your joy and happiness pour out. Breathe deeply, sing or shout if you feel like it.

You don't always have to visualize the same fountain. If you want, you can visualize a different or modified one every day. What counts is that you remain firmly convinced of its rejuvenating properties.

CHAPTER 12

Dealing with Everyday Problems

Pain? Never Heard of it!

What is pain? In physiological terms, it's a message that travels from the nerve endings up the spine to the cerebral cortex in the brain. The brain then releases pain-suppressing substances called endorphines, which come to our aid. Pain, whether from a wound, a chronic illness or our body's reaction to a harmful substance, is part of our daily lives. Analgesics (painkillers) are the most frequently prescribed pharmaceutical products in the Western world. Who among us can claim never to have taken aspirin or codeine?

But it's not good to eliminate all pain – it may be the symptom of a problem that must be treated more carefully. If you get rid of the pain, it doesn't necessarily mean that you get rid of the cause of the problem.

But whatever the cause of the pain, it is possible to soothe it and even to make it disappear. The first method you already know since it was described in Chapter 6. If you've forgotten it, turn back and read it again.

There's another technique which is just as effective, based on the principles of self-hypnosis. It's time to get out the tape recorder again.

ANTI-PAIN: A GENERAL METHOD

Go back to the section on stress in Chapter 11 (p. 84). There you will find the two processes of descending and ascending described in detail.

These two processes are separated by an intermediate process, which can be modified at will to fight a given problem. In Chapter 11 the problem was stress. Here it's pain.

Now turn on your tape recorder.

Step one: descending   See Chapter 11.

Step two: anti-pain

1. Give your pain a form, for example a tunnel. Imagine yourself entering the tunnel. The pain intensifies for a few seconds. You start walking through the tunnel. You see the light of day at the far end, and each step brings you closer to it. The more you advance, the less pain you feel.
2. The circle of light grows larger little by little. You feel better and better. With each step you take, your pain diminishes.
3. You feel more and more at ease. You're relaxed, serene. The pain is almost imperceptible. The circle of light at the end of the tunnel grows larger. You're almost there.
4. You control the tunnel. You can make it longer or shorter at will. Every time you're in pain, you can use it. When you come out the other end, your pain is soothed and you feel good.

Step three: ascending

1. Once again turn to Chapter 11 and look at the technique described there.

You now possess a general method which can be applied to any kind of pain.

ANTI-PAIN: A SPECIFIC METHOD

Of course, you are free to adapt this general method to more specific kinds of pain: wounds, diseases, post-operative pains, stress pain, fatigue, chronic pain, accidental bruises, strains etc. Just remember that you must:

- Repeat key phrases by modifying them to suit the situation
- Use simple vocabulary, with lots of images

- Impress your subconscious with images of accomplished success
- Place a time limit on all references to the future (for example, 'In a few minutes I will . . .' or 'As soon as I've done this I'll feel . . .' etc.)
- Indicate the beginning and end of each of your actions.

The processes of descending and ascending remain the same. You attack a specific pain by creating an appropriate image for the intermediate stage. Here are a few examples.

Pain caused by a wound or an operation

1. Imagine your pain in the form of a large red, flaming ball. Concentrate on it and imagine it decreasing in size, like a planet that's getting further and further away. It appears less full and more dull and lacklustre.
2. As the sphere diminishes in size, so does your pain. The sphere gets smaller and smaller, clearer and clearer. Your pain is getting weaker and weaker. Look at the ball – it's almost disappeared.
3. The ball is now minuscule, of a translucent pink colour. You feel hardly any more pain. The ball keeps getting more distant, and you feel no more pain. You can't see it at all now. You feel good, relaxed, free of all your pain. You are relieved and happy.

Chronic pain, or pain caused by disease

Let's say, for example, that you suffer from rheumatoid arthritis. You can use the following imagery:

1. Concentrate on the part of your body that is causing you most pain. Feel the pain in your swollen joints.
2. Relax the muscles around the joints. A jet of clear water flows over your joints. It washes them, purifies them and strengthens them. And it carries away your pain. You see the cool water pouring over your fingers, your knees, your shoulders. It calms you, and makes the inflammation disappear. You start to feel soothing relief. Your joints relax. You can move them painlessly.
3. From now on, your subconscious will start working to keep the pain from coming back. You are liberated. Your joints are supple, the swelling is completely gone.

USING AFFIRMATIONS

You can also successfully fight pain caused by chronic illness by using the Coué method, based on auto-suggestion, described on pp. 73–4.

A FINAL WARNING

Effective as they may be, these self-analgesic techniques do not replace treatment if you are unaware of the origin of the pain. If you suffer from persistent pains of unknown origin, consult a doctor.

How to Handle Nervousness

If you're a nervy, irritable person, you're not only poisoning your own existence but also the existence of those around you. You get nervy about trivial matters, and you live in a state of perpetual tension. You're easily upset: the slightest problem can make you lose your cool.

At first, your friends try to be patient and understanding. But gradually they will become less and less affectionate as they tire of your outbursts. Tolerance has its limits.

Sooner or later you'll probably start suffering from hypertension, gastric ulcers, constipation, migraines, insomnia, arteriosclerosis and other unpleasant disorders, some more serious than others. It's time to calm down!

YOUR MENTAL RETREAT IS THERAPEUTIC

You've learnt to use your mental sanctuary as a base for all your relaxation, visualization, meditation, breathing and self-hypnosis exercises. But your sanctuary is therapeutic in itself. You've chosen it and designed it to your taste. It's your decompression chamber, an oasis of peace and harmony. It represents the best of yourself. Take full advantage of it. Visit your sanctuary at least once a day. Whether you're at the office, on the bus or at home, use any spare moments you have to benefit from your sanctuary.

GET RID OF YOUR TENSIONS

There's a place in Iceland where powerful hot springs of boiling, sulphurous water erupt at regular intervals. The region is called Geyser, from which comes the name for this type of spring.

This exercise consists of visualizing your nervousness like a geyser.

1. Get comfortable in your mental sanctuary.
2. Imagine that the tension you feel is a column of white, foaming water that surges up suddenly to the top of your skull.
3. With each surge you feel liberated. The geyser evaporates into the air, and your nervousness dissipates along with it. You feel all the tension released, and your nervousness is gone.

EXERCISE FOR CALMING YOUR NERVES

This exercise is based on a principle whose effectiveness you'll probably already have discovered: the soothing quality of your own natural rhythm.

1. Imagine you're on a beach, at night. The stars begin shining, the sand feels cool under your body. The night is beautiful, and you feel good.
2. Look at the ocean.
3. Every three or four seconds a wave rises up, foaming at its crest, and breaks gently on the beach.
4. Visualize this process a number of times. Divide the 'life' of each wave into three stages: formation, appearance of foam and breaking on the beach. Watch a dozen or so waves as they break a few yards from where you're sitting.

These exercises should enable you to get rid of your aggressiveness and calm your nerves. They are well worth the effort. If you're not concerned about your own wellbeing, then think of those around you.

Stomach and Intestines

SOME ESSENTIAL PSYCHOLOGICAL 'REPAIRS'

Do you often get stomach aches? Do you have difficulty digesting your food? Do you suffer from constipation or its opposite, chronic diarrhoea? Well, there's one consolation – you're not alone.

Gastric problems, which we group under the name 'indigestion', as well as the uncontrolled malfunctioning of our intestines, may be the result of a serious problem which requires professional medical treatment. Once again, pain is an alarm signal which we send to our brain. Ignoring the cause and being satisfied with just eliminating the pain can have disastrous consequences.

However it frequently happens that, despite the absence of any serious physical ailment, we will suffer from gastro-intestinal problems which are sufficiently serious to make life unpleasant. These kinds of disorders are frequently of psychological origin. For example, if you don't like your work you might have trouble digesting your breakfast. If you are under a lot of stress, or you're worried about something, then don't be surprised if your intestines literally turn to liquid every two or three hours.

Do you know why a surprisingly high number of women suffer from chronic constipation? Certain psychologists believe that the cause of the problem lies in our inherited cultural values:

- 'Ladies' were not supposed to admit that they had to go to the toilet.
- Offices and other public buildings were originally designed for men, and did not have women's toilet facilities, since very few women worked outside the home. So women who began working constipated themselves by holding back all day long.

Gastro-intestinal symptoms of benign and purely psychological origin are easy to eliminate with the help of a few exercises.

Exercise to improve digestion

To relieve abdominal pain it is sometimes necessary to unblock the solar plexus, which is situated just behind the stomach and a little below the diaphragm.

1. Get comfortable in your mental retreat.
2. Do a relaxation exercise. For example, try to recall a pleasant experience that happened to you a few days before – a walk in the forest, a session at the gym, a massage, a visit to a theatre etc. Avoid any sensations related to eating or food.
3. Try to recall everything you felt during the enjoyable experience. Bask in the feeling of wellbeing you experienced.
4. Once you're completely relaxed, imagine a golden disc a few inches above your solar plexus. Hundreds of energy rays emanate from this disc and bombard your solar plexus. They clean it, massage it, unblock it.
5. In a few minutes you should start feeling the soothing effects of the exercise. The tension that is preventing you from digesting food, or

which is upsetting the smooth functioning of your intestines, is beginning to dissolve.

6. Be careful not to make this 'bombardment' last more than a few minutes. The effect of this exercise is relatively powerful, and must be applied prudently.

Exercise to eliminate toxins

Have you ever had the impression that your system was fouled up, like a chimney encrusted with soot? Are your intestinal irregularities and stomach pains sending you a message that your digestive mechanism is suffering from some kind of virus? As its name suggests, this exercise will help you clean out your 'plumbing' system, get rid of toxins and at the same time help you relax.

1. As usual, get comfortable in your mental sanctuary. Now imagine that a fresh water spring starts flowing from a rock just above you.
2. It bathes you from head to toe. You feel as if you were standing under a cool, refreshing cascade.
3. Feel the water flowing over you. Breathe it, drink a few mouthfuls.
4. Enjoy the pleasure of standing under the cleansing waterfall for a few moments.
5. Now imagine that the water enters your system through the crown of your head. It flows slowly through your organism. You feel your chest area purified as the fresh, cool water bathes your lungs. You feel incredibly good and pure.
6. The water flows down to your stomach and cleans it out completely. Then it moves into the large intestine, down through the small intestine and out through the rectum. Feel it purifying and relaxing your organs.
7. After a moment, close up the spring. The water stops flowing. Remain still for a few moments, with your eyes closed, before coming back to reality.

Always meditate

Meditation exercises are among the most effective for regulating your digestive functions. Their effects are probably less intense than those of the other methods just described, but they are perhaps more durable. Any kind of meditation will help, whether you do hypno-meditation, repetition of a mantra or any of the techniques in earlier chapters. What is important is to attain a transcendental state. When you come out of a meditation period, you will feel so much better that problems like tension, stress, lassitude, anxiety and any digestive disorders will have much less of an effect on you.

Put a Stop to Migraines

Someone who has never suffered from a pulsating migraine headache is incapable of understanding the horror of this kind of piercing, overpowering pain, which batters the skull, provokes nausea and vomiting, and is aggravated by the slightest noise, light or movement. In some persons, bright light during a migraine attack can even cause double vision. Why do some people suffer from migraines?

An excess of certain toxic substances – sweets, chocolate, fried food, alcohol and tobacco – tends to bring them on. People who eat a lot of meat are often subject to rather strong headaches, but they rarely reach the stage of a migraine. Certain food additives, too, are suspected of causing migraines. So have another look at what you eat, and take any measures that are appropriate.

Eyestrain, bad posture at work, or spending long hours in front of a badly adjusted computer screen can also cause pulsating migraines.

But more often than not, migraines are signals sent by our subconscious. There are two typical migraine situations:

- When we have to attend a function (dinner party, family affair, meeting etc.) that we really don't want to, or which disrupts our initial plans, forcing us to be with people we'd rather not see.
- When we are apprehensive about something, or downright afraid. For example, the fear of not being able to accomplish a certain task, or the fear of being hurt, fear of flying, fear that someone we love will abandon us, fear of an exam etc.

PREVENTION

USE THE BLACKBOARD–WHITE BOARD METHOD

Start by examining your lifestyle and eating habits (see above). Take any appropriate measures to eliminate possible causes of migraines.

Do you remember the blackboard–white board method on p. 28? This is a perfect occasion to put it to good use.

1. At night, when you go to bed, write a question on the blackboard: 'Why do I get migraines?' If you remember your last attack, make the question more precise: 'Why did I get a migraine on that day?'
2. Go to sleep, expecting to find the answer on the white board when you awaken.
3. The next morning, visualize the white board. You may be surprised by the answer you find written on it. The migraine you had was like a fine that your subconscious made you pay after judging your behaviour.

You may not discover the cause of your migraine right away. Persevere by using the blackboard–white board method for twenty-one days.

Positive self image technique

You can also work on the problem by applying the technique of developing a positive self image. Here's how to proceed:

1. Find a photograph of yourself, one that you like, where you're smiling, happy, carefree and healthy.
2. At least three times a day, sit down to do the breathing exercises described in Chapter 6.
3. During the exercises, look at the photograph and impress your mind with this image of yourself, happy and trouble free.

WHAT TO DO DURING AN ATTACK

It's more difficult to get rid of a migraine than to prevent one from occurring, once you've found out what the cause is. But here are two visualization exercises that have proved effective.

Exercise to suppress migraine pain instantly

1. Ask a friend or family member to help you.
2. Get comfortable, dim the lights, close the door and try to relax as much as possible.
3. Now the person helping you should ask the following questions:
   - If your migraine had a geometric form, what would it be?
   - If your migraine had a colour, what would it be?
   - If your migraine were a receptacle, how much water would it hold?

4. Then the person helping you starts again, asking the same series of questions.

People who have tried this exercise usually begin with the answers: a circle, bright red, X number of pints. With each repetition the answers change. The form of the circle becomes a square, then a triangle, then a rectangle, and then goes back to a circle. The colour goes from bright red to blue, to green, to orange and finally to a pale pink. The volume diminishes progressively from a few pints to half a pint, to a glass and finally to a spoonful.

When your migraine has been reduced to a pale pink sphere, no larger than a spoonful of water, it will have completely disappeared.

Exercise to relax your brain

1. Get comfortable in a quiet place, preferably your mental retreat.
2. Create a mental image of your brain inside your skull.
3. Now do a special breathing exercise: with each intake of breath, imagine that your brain expands and lightly touches your skull.
4. With each expiration, it resumes its normal size. Repeat the process a number of times – the results will surprise you!

Colds and Snuffles

Have you noticed that some people never seem to catch colds, while people around them spend the winter coughing, sniffling and sneezing? People who don't catch cold have a few things in common:

- They consume enough vitamin C (at least 3 grams per day).
- They play outdoor sports, or at least enjoy spending winter days outdoors (dressed suitably, of course).
- They don't usually smoke.
- They seem to be psychologically fulfilled.

On the other hand, you will notice that people who suffer from chronic coughs, laryngitis, colds and flu are often frustrated, and not very happy in their family lives. They tend to let others take advantage of them. They are generally seen as submissive, and so it's not surprising that they are often depressed.

How to Get Rid of a Cold Fast

Here's a very simple technique that you can apply as soon as you feel the first symptoms of a cold coming on. Do it at least three times a day: you should get rid of your cold in twenty-four hours.

1. Squeeze an orange and a lemon. You can also add a grapefruit if you like. Dissolve 1 gram of vitamin C in the juice.
2. Go to your mental retreat.
3. Practise rhythmic breathing, while concentrating on the sensations in your head.
4. After a few minutes, return from your sanctuary and drink the juice.

Getting Rid of a Cough

Sometimes a wicked little cough will persist after a cold or flu is over. The throat remains irritated, disturbing your sleep (and that of your partner).

1. Go to your mental retreat.
2. Do your rhythmic breathing exercises, concentrating on the sensations in your throat.
3. Visualize the inside of your throat – normally it's a smooth passageway, but now it's covered with a multitude of sharp little stones.
4. Next, visualize a wave of golden light around your neck, like a scarf. It slowly penetrates into your throat.
5. The golden light spreads along the whole throat passage, causing the sharp stones to disappear in its path.
6. After a few minutes, the passageway is completely smooth. The golden light passes through your skin and out of your throat. It remains for a few minutes, wrapped around your neck like a scarf, and then disappears.

Forget About New Year Flu

It's a little harder to get rid of a flu than a cold. The symptoms are usually more serious, and last longer. But if you want to avoid coming down with flu, as so often happens around Christmas-time, you can use this three-step method of self-hypnosis (like the technique you learnt in Chapter 11). Record the following instructions on your tape recorder.

First step: descending

Second step

1. Relax, while concentrating on getting better. Imagine that your entire body, from the crown of your skull right down to your toes, is filled with an orange colour, as if you'd become a huge glass of orange juice. Now imagine that you're pulling a plug, situated under the soles of your feet.
2. The orange colour empties out slowly, carrying with it the infection, all the microbes that are making you ill. Feel the liquid flowing out of your body, as if you were pouring one glass of orange juice into another. Little by little, your body empties itself of the orange colour.
3. Now a beautiful golden colour enters your body through the soles of your feet. It rises slowly up to the crown of your skull, filling you with health and wellbeing. Feel the beautiful golden wave charging you with fresh energy. It spreads throughout your entire body, healing you completely.

Third step: ascending

Ouch! My Back!

It is estimated that about a third of the population suffers from back problems. Why do we get back pains? Simply because we treat our backs badly. We strain our posture at work, we spend too much time behind the wheel of the car, we sleep on bad mattresses and we fail to align our shoulders and trunk properly.

It has also been observed that a lack of harmony in day-to-day life, the obligation of bearing heavy emotional burdens, stress and suppressed anger, frequently result in terrible back pains.

Generally, back pain caused by bad posture is situated along the spine, in the lumbar region. Psychological problems, especially stress, tend to affect the trapezoid region (shoulders and upper back) as well as the neck. This is more a muscular problem than a bone disorder.

So if you suffer from back pain, begin by taking the following measures:

- Look at your chairs and your bed. You can buy orthopaedic chairs and mattresses which are designed to support the spine.

- Learn to do physical exercises which strengthen your trapezoidal, abdominal and upper leg muscles. Both your health and physical appearance will benefit.
- Analyse your lifestyle, and find out what might be causing psychological and/or emotional problems. Don't hesitate to consult a professional for help if you feel you can't find a way out of the situation yourself.
- Lastly, once a day do a relaxation session, accompanied by the following exercise.

EXERCISE TO SOOTHE YOUR VERTEBRAE

1. Retreat to your mental sanctuary.
2. Start by doing some rhythmic breathing, concentrating on the part of your back that's especially painful (trapezoid muscle, cervical vertebrae, lumbar vertebrae, kidney area etc.).
3. After a few minutes, visualize a concentrated and powerful ray of white light, originating in space, as it beams directly in on the painful area. You feel it warming your vertebrae, your muscles, your bones.
4. Count to ten, breathing deeply. The ray of light dissolves. Continuing breathing and open your eyes.
5. The pain should be gone.

One small warning: this is a very intense exercise, so don't apply the ray of light for more than ten seconds.

You can also work on your back pain using the three-step technique of self-hypnosis described on p. 118, following the method for alleviating chronic pain.

But be careful. Just because the exercise removes your pain momentarily doesn't mean that you can neglect taking corrective measures to remedy the cause of the problem. It would be a pity if you overlooked something as simple as changing your office chair so that you sit straighter and more comfortably when working, just because you were able to soothe your pain with self-hypnosis and visualization.

Regaining Sexual Energy

As you may know, sexual energy is nothing but the transformation of mental energy, thanks to imagination. . . . If you feel you lack sexual energy, whether you're a man or a woman, start by examining certain aspects of your life:

- Do you eat properly? A deficiency of vitamins and/or minerals can have a debilitating effect on sexual desire.
- Do you do enough exercise? There is ample proof that a person in good physical condition is much less likely to suffer from impotence or frigidity.
- Are you aware of your bio-rhythm? We don't all enjoy making love at the same time of day. It's possible that you and your partner prefer entirely different times. If that's the case, dicuss the problem and look for a compromise solution.
- Do you know how to relax? Three-quarters of the population don't know how to relax. That's why we should make relaxation exercises a part of our daily routine. A good rule to follow: don't make love to relax — but relax to make love.

After looking at all these factors, you may want to do the following exercise which will teach you to channel your mental and spiritual energy so that it is transformed into sexual energy. The technique takes effect gradually.

EXERCISE FOR LIBERATING SEXUAL ENERGY

1. As usual, retreat to your mental sanctuary.
2. Try to give mental energy a discernible form. You can choose any form you like, as long as it's perfectly comprehensible to your subconscious: a waterfall, an avalanche, a majestic river, a ray of light, a shower of meteorites . . . it's entirely up to you.
3. Now imagine that the form you decided on penetrates your system through the crown of your skull. You feel it spreading through your head. It fills all the recesses of your brain.
4. Still visualizing the form of the energy, make it descend to your throat. It's so powerful that you feel it expanding your throat.
5. Next the energy descends into your solar plexus. This region, situated a little below the diaphragm, is extremely important. You feel the energy filling your abdominal region.
6. The last step consists of sending the energy to where you suspect it is lacking, i.e. your genital area. Imagine the energy flooding the lower portion of your body for a few minutes.

Doing this exercise regularly each day for twenty-one days will release an enormous store of sexual energy into your system.

Suppress Your Allergies

Whether your allergies are inherited, psychosomatic or caused by external factors, you can get rid of them by taking the following measures:

- Adopt a positive outlook. Read over the section on optimism at the beginning of Chapter 11.
- Try to eliminate stress factors from your life, or at least minimize them. Don't hesitate to consult a psychologist or a psychotherapist.
- Lead a healthy life (proper nutrition, exercise, restorative sleep etc.).
- Use the technique of self-hypnosis described below.

EXERCISE TO CLEAR THE LUNGS

Tape the following instructions on your cassette recorder:

First step: descending

Second step

1. Breathe deeply and more and more easily. Stop breathing a moment, then take a deep breath. Now exhale deeply. Stop a moment . . . and so on.
2. Imagine that you're breathing clean, pure air – the air you find at the seashore, full of sea spray, or the crystalline air of a mountaintop, covered with snow. The air is plentiful, refreshing, clean, comforting and beneficial.
3. Now imagine that you're walking in a pine forest. You breathe the fragrant air, charged with beneficial particles which enter your sinuses and clean them. You breathe deeply. You feel marvellously well.
4. From now on, each time you smell or see a substance to which you are allergic, you will visualize the mountain, the ocean or the pine forest, and you will relax by deeply inhaling the pure,

fragrant air. You will feel your sinuses and lungs fill with pure, incredibly pure air. You breathe freely, deeply.

Third step: ascending

You can also treat asthma with this technique. Replace the beginning of the last paragraph with 'Whenever you feel an asthma attack coming on . . .'.

CHAPTER · 13

Putting an End to Phobias

If someone asked you for a definition of 'phobia', what would your answer be? Most people would say that it's a fear, a kind of anxiety or irrational aversion. Actually, phobias are far from being irrational. There are thousands of kinds of phobia, each possessing a very precise cause which a psychologist or psychotherapist would be very capable of bringing to the surface. How do you know if you're suffering from a phobia?

In general, phobias produce easily identifiable physical symptoms – for example trembling, cold sweats, shaking and nausea. Everyone knows the expression, 'My hair stood on end!' This is how many people feel when asked to describe the way in which the object of their phobia affects them.

From a psychological point of view, if the phobia is serious enough it can become an obsession and damage relationships with those close to you, your productivity at work, the quality of your sleep and your digestion.

How to Treat any Phobia

Before looking at specific methods for current phobias and fears, here is a generalized technique which aims to make your subconscious impervious to phobias of all kinds. If you suffer from a particular phobia, it would be wise to combine the two types of exercises.

The objective of the first method is to instil confidence in yourself, whatever the situation. It is based on the self-hypnosis exercise, which has already been mentioned on several occasions – only this time you will be confronting your fear head on.

So get your tape recorder ready, and proceed as you've been instructed to do in the section on self-hypnosis.

EXERCISE FOR DEVELOPING YOUR STRENGTH

First step: descending

Second step

1. Imagine yourself face to face with the object of your fear. Give it a form. You see it clearly. Look at it, and realize just how weak it really is. You are much stronger than it is. Your phobia is afraid of you because you are so much stronger. You feel relaxed, perfectly calm and sure of your strength. You smile, because your fear has lost all its strength and is no longer important.
2. You don't care about it any more; it doesn't interest you in the least. Your life will be so much more pleasant without it. You can face any situation, because you possess such immense strength.
3. From now on, whenever you feel anxious you will breathe deeply, you will relax, and you will feel a current of strength run through you.
4. You are happy. Your fear has vanished. You are strong and powerful. You have complete confidence in yourself.

Third step: ascending

ADAPT THE METHOD TO YOUR PARTICULAR PHOBIA

In this section you will learn about specific methods to combat the most common kinds of phobia. There's nothing to prevent you from adapting them to your own phobia, even if it isn't mentioned here.

Intangible Phobias

Phobias can be divided into intangible ones (such as a fear of death, or of speaking in public) and concrete ones (such as snakes or mice). Let's deal first with the intangible ones.

Stop Being Afraid of Illness

A phobia about getting ill (pathophobia) is common among people who were very ill during childhood, or who come from families with a history of hereditary illness. The object of this method is to instil in you a perpetual sense of wellbeing and invulnerability. By conditioning your subconscious through self-hypnosis, you become protected against illness.

First step: descending

Second step

- You are in good health, there is no trace of disease in your body. You look at yourself in the mirror. You're happy. Your skin is radiant, your eyes are brimming with health. You feel perfectly fit. You're full of energy. Life is interesting and beautiful. You're very happy. Everything is going well. Your body is healthy, perfectly healthy.

Third step: ascending

Are You Afraid of Getting Old or Dying?

If so, don't be ashamed. We're all afraid of ageing, because we associate it with decline. And we're afraid of death because it represents the unknown – a place from which we cannot return. We're afraid of suffering before we die, and of finding ourselves alone at the moment of death.

The fear of ageing and death (thanatophobia) is one of the main characteristics which separate us from animals. It's the price we have to pay for belonging to a 'superior species'.

Did you know that in our dreams and fantasies we always have an image of ourselves as being young, despite our real age? The fact that the subconscious entirely refutes the idea of ageing can be of great help in conditioning our conscious minds as well!

ANTI-WRINKLE EXERCISE

1. Retreat to your mental sanctuary.
2. Once you are perfectly relaxed, imagine yourself a few years in

the future, looking exactly the same as you do today, with few wrinkles and no grey hair.

3. When this image is firmly established in your mind, imagine yourself doing one of your favourite activities with as much energy and enthusiasm as you have today. Visualize yourself in the company of people who are younger than you are. They are listening to you, they compliment you, joke with you.

4. Even if your present health is not good, or if you're a few pounds overweight, you should imagine yourself in excellent health, trim and fit.

In other words, do as much as you can to counteract the effects of ageing. Do the fountain of youth exercise (see pp. 89–90) regularly. Stimulate your body with regular physical exercise, and your mind with work, study, travel, hobbies and discussion.

Tobacco and alcohol age the body prematurely, as do vitamin and mineral deficiencies.

Never say, 'I don't do this kind of thing at my age.' Keep dressing young, wearing fun clothes. If you find life interesting, if you take pleasure in what life has to offer, then the fear of ageing will disappear and you'll think less and less about death.

Fear of Lacking Money

If you're afraid to the point of panic about being poor, about suddenly finding yourself in dire straits, don't worry. Your problem is not uncommon, and even has a name: peniophobia.

In general, this phobia is present to a greater or lesser extent throughout the lives of persons who experienced serious financial problems during their childhood. On the other hand, people who face financial problems as adults seem much less concerned with the idea of suddenly losing everything once they've acquired a certain affluence.

A conditioning process using self-hypnosis can cure you of this obsession, which can ruin your life and label you a miser among your friends.

ANTI-POVERTY CONDITIONING

First step: descending

Second step

1. Give a form to poverty, for example a soiled and torn piece of clothing. Look at it, stare at it. It does not make you afraid. It can't do anything to you. You are the strong one. You can do whatever you want with it – throw it in the dustbin, tear it up into a thousand pieces.
2. Poverty can't hurt you. You are its master. It has no power over you, just like that piece of torn and dirty clothing that means nothing to you and is worth absolutely nothing. You don't fear it, because you're stronger than it is.
3. From now on you won't be afraid of not having enough money. Poverty can't touch you. You are vastly stronger than it is. You won't even think about it, because it isn't worth the effort. You're strong and you're happy.

Third step: ascending

The Spectre of Jealousy

You love someone, and you're afraid of losing them. That's very normal. But it can happen – and you've surely seen cases – where this fear can be transformed into obsession and even hate. It manifests itself as a totally exaggerated jealousy, which may upset your partner so much that the relationship is destroyed and you lose the person you love. How can you avoid this?

The simplest and most effective method for getting rid of these unhealthy thoughts is, once again, the black and white boards.

ANTI-JEALOUSY EXERCISE

1. Get comfortable in your mental retreat, and visualize the two boards as well as the hammer.
2. Write your negative thoughts on the blackboard. For example, 'She's going to leave me. . .' or 'I don't think she loves me any more. . .' or 'I don't trust her. . .' or 'I should read her mail. . .' or

—— 111 ——

'I'll ask questions about the people she knows. . .' or 'I'll follow him. . .' or 'I'm afraid he'll meet someone else. . .' etc.

3. Remember that you must make these thoughts appear very distinctly in your visualization, written in white chalk on the blackboard. When you've finished, step back and read what you've written.

4. Now destroy the blackboard with the hammer. Get angry, use all your force, all your hate, to smash it to bits. All your resentment and fears should be channelled into this destructive action.

5. Calm yourself. Do a few breathing exercises and relax.

6. Now turn to the white board. Write down your positive thoughts with a blue or black marker: 'I trust him. . .', 'I won't be afraid she'll leave me. . .', 'I won't listen in to his telephone conversations any more. . .', 'I believe everything he tells me about what he does. . .', 'I know she loves me as much as I love her. . .' and so on.

7. Read these thoughts over a few times. Allow a feeling of love and contentment to spread through you. Imagine your new attitude and behaviour as something that is already accomplished. Immerse yourself in your positive thoughts. Impress them deeply into your subconscious.

If you like, use the twenty-one-day technique, which you already know. It will give you the time you need to strengthen your new attitude, and to anchor the positive images more deeply in your subconscious.

If you still feel you're not completely 'cured' of your hate, turn to the three-month programme. If you recall, this simply means practising the exercise for twenty-one days, then taking a week's break before starting another twenty-one-day cycle, and so on for three months.

Are You Afraid of Approaching the Opposite Sex?

While we're on the subject of interpersonal relations, are you excessively shy when approaching the opposite sex? This kind of fear is getting more and more rare in today's world. Co-ed schools, and the acceptance of women as part of the workforce, has resulted, among other things, in making relations between the sexes more natural and relaxed.

But if you think you suffer from this phobia, you're not alone. There's nothing especially repulsive about your personality or appearance – you just haven't been able to find the right person for you, your 'soulmate'. Don't worry – there are steps you can take to remedy the situation.

There are two solid methods for increasing your self-confidence, and for getting rid of any complexes that can prevent you from being happy. The first exercise is a very simple visualization.

FINDING YOUR SOULMATE

1. Get comfortable in your mental retreat.
2. Now imagine that someone is coming. If your sanctuary is a room, you hear a knock at the door. If you're outside, say in a forest clearing, you hear the snapping of branches underfoot; and so on. Before you actually see the person who is arriving, you experience a pleasant sensation.
3. Then you see the person, who can be completely imaginary, or someone you're already attracted to but whom you haven't dared approach. The important thing is to feel attracted to that person when you see him or her – both to their physical appearance and to their personality.
4. Go up to the visitor and take their hand. Feel the heat of their palm against yours.
5. Now show them your sanctuary. Describe all the little details. If you're outside, ask your visitor to breathe in the fragrant smells of nature. If you're in a room, admire together the furnishings, the view, the design of the room etc.
6. When the tour is over, sit down with your visitor and share a drink or something to eat.
7. Then leave together, calmly. Open your eyes and breathe deeply.

If you practise this exercise once a day for a few weeks, you should get rid of most of your apprehensions concerning the opposite sex. If you feel you need to do some follow-up exercises because your new-found confidence is still a bit fragile, then imagine yourself sharing your favourite pastimes with the other person.

Sharing a meal together is especially effective, due to the almost sacred aura that our society places around the ritual of eating.

You can also use a self-hypnosis technique similar to the one that follows.

EXERCISE TO COMMUNICATE YOUR FEELINGS

First step: descending

Second step

1. Imagine that you meet someone with all the qualities you appreciate in a person. You have common interests, you like each other, and there is a very strong mutual attraction. You're made for each other.
2. You know how to communicate your feelings to this other person. You understand him (or her) and he understands you. You have no fear of approaching the person and telling him you were made for each other.
3. You can be intimate. Being close to the other person is pleasant. He or she does not frighten you. You are ready to start a fulfilling relationship. You're happy to love someone.
4. From now on, you won't be afraid to approach someone you feel attracted to. You are strong. You are ready to love, and to be loved in return.

Third step: ascending

Fear of Getting Attached

The technique just described can also be used in the case of someone who isn't afraid to approach members of the opposite sex, but is afraid of falling in love and forming a lasting attachment to someone. This fear, called amorophobia, is especially common among people who have already experienced a failed relationship, or who are obsessed by the idea of being rejected. If you're one of these people you might want to consult a psychologist or psychotherapist in addition to practising your exercises. In a few sessions a trained professional should be able to restore the confidence you lack in yourself, show you how to inspire lasting love in someone, and teach you how to deal with that kind of love yourself.

Fear of Pregnancy and Giving Birth

Whether this phobia is caused by a previous painful experience, or whether deep down you've always been afraid of giving birth, it can be got rid of.

IF YOU'RE NOT PREGNANT YET

At this stage, the best way to get rid of your apprehension is through relaxation, accompanied by positive thoughts such as:

- 'I want to get pregnant. . .'
- 'I look forward to being pregnant. . .'
- 'I will be happy to be pregnant. . .' and so on.

You can also use the black and white board method. On the blackboard write your negative thoughts, such as:

- 'I am afraid of pregnancy. . .'
- 'I don't want my body to get deformed. . .'
- 'I hate feeling sick. . .'
- 'I'm afraid I won't know how to take care of the baby. . .' and so on.

On the white board, write your encouraging thoughts:

- 'I'm so happy at the thought of expecting a baby. . .'
- 'My relationship is going extremely well. . .'
- 'I will not suffer from morning sickness. . .'
- 'I'll get back into perfect shape after giving birth. . .'

A cycle of twenty-one days should be enough to get rid of your apprehensions about pregnancy. If not, continue with a three-month cycle.

IF YOU'RE ALREADY PREGNANT

You're waiting to give birth, but you're very apprehensive. You are not aware that the more you're afraid, the more sickness you'll suffer, and the more susceptible you'll be to developing premature contractions which could keep you in bed for the rest of your term. Not a very pleasant scenario.

- To calm yourself, retreat to your mental sanctuary on a regular basis and spend some time there.
- Do breathing exercises regularly. Use the relaxation method you prefer at least once a day.
- Don't neglect to attend your ante-natal classes. As well as providing you with information, they offer the opportunity to meet other couples who are also awaiting a baby. You know how reassuring it can be when you're apprehensive about something, to talk about it with someone who is in a similar situation.
- Don't hide your fears from your partner under the pretext that a

'real woman' should not be afraid of pregnancy and birth. Confide in him. Sharing your fear is half the battle of getting rid of it.

- Finally, do the following self-hypnosis exercise regularly:

First step: descending

Second step

1. Imagine yourself in your mental sanctuary. All is calm and peaceful. You are rested, you feel good, and so does your baby. Let yourself bask in the gentleness of the moment, and in the love you feel for your baby. Pause for a moment.
2. Think about how much you want to have this baby. You have so much love to give. Imagine your love as a golden light which surrounds the baby and protects it. See the light inside you. Now pause again.
3. Talk to your baby. Tell him (or her) that you love him, that you're waiting for his arrival with joy, that you'll be so happy when he finally arrives. Imagine that the baby hears and understands you, and is smiling at you. Relax completely. Imagine that you're giving birth on (insert the predicted date). You start to feel the contractions, and you immediately begin doing the breathing exercises that you have learnt in your ante-natal classes. You know exactly what to do when the contractions start.
4. Imagine the actual birth. You push, you breathe, you think of your baby and you talk to him. You feel fine, the baby hears you, he wants to come out and smile at you. You continue breathing. And you relax. You're not afraid.
5. You're proud of yourself. You know how to relax and do the breathing you were taught. The birth goes extremely well. Everyone around you is happy. The baby is all right – you continue pushing to help him out. You're happy and relaxed. Everything's fine.

Third stage: ascending

What's interesting about this exercise is that you can practise it right up to the last minute, along with the breathing exercises from your ante-natal classes.

It will also help you avoid post partum depression, because before giving birth you will already have got used to the idea of having your baby with you. You'll be calmer, more relaxed, less inclined to feel that events are out of your control. And you will start producing milk more easily and more abundantly.

The Fear of Living

It's completely normal to feel depressed sometimes. However, if you feel that depression is becoming your predominant state of mind, if you feel apathetic and can't sleep enough (at least six or seven hours a night), or on the contrary if all you want to do is sleep (nine or ten hours a night), if you've lost your appetite or if you eat too much (especially sweets), if you're tired when you get up in the morning, if you don't feel capable of generating the least enthusiasm or sexual desire, then it's time to do something about it. You're on the road to chronic depression.

EXERCISE

It has recently been discovered that one of the best antidotes for depression is physical exercise. Doing regular exercise modifies the brain chemistry. It is physiologically impossible to be depressed while engaged in sports, just as it's physiologically impossible to get ill while you're laughing.

PRACTISE MEDITATION

Read Chapter 8 and start yourself on a regular meditation programme. Whatever method you choose, meditation is a highly effective anti-depressant. It frees you from your fears about life, from being afraid of your responsibilities, from pessimism, or from any suicidal thoughts that might enter your mind. It's obvious that anyone who is susceptible to pessimism is a perfect candidate for depression. Read the beginning of Chapter 11 again. Answer the questions there, and then for a period of a few weeks do the exercises aimed at eliminating negative thoughts.

A SELF-HYPNOSIS TECHNIQUE

First step: descending

Second step

1. You feel good, very good. Your life is going extremely well. You have no reason to be afraid. You don't feel at all depressed. You're optimistic. You have confidence in the future, you are loved by those close to you, your colleagues respect you. You're good at your work. You have nothing to worry about.
2. You're relaxed and happy. You feel fine.
3. Starting today, you will not be afraid of the future. You'll feel strong. You will be the master of your own destiny. You have absolutely no reason to be afraid. The future belongs to you. You are happy, loved and respected.

Third step: ascending

Of course if, after a certain amount of time and despite all your personal efforts, your depression persists, you should look for outside help. Consult a hypnotherapist or psychotherapist who can help you discover the underlying causes of your fears, and show you how to cure them.

Do You Suffer from Vertigo?

Most people don't find themselves having to walk on the window ledge of a twenty-storey building. However, vertigo can strike at any time – on an escalator or a balcony, even crossing a bridge. If you're subject to vertigo you can apply a very simple self-hypnosis technique, which will provide you with a feeling of strength and mastery of the situation.

Before turning on your tape recorder, try to recall a pleasant experience from your past.

First step: descending

Second step

1. Think about everything you've accomplished in the past. Think about your strong points. You can go wherever you want. Now

recall a place where you felt happy and peaceful. The same feeling of peace and happiness will appear when you find yourself in a high place. You are calm. You feel fine. You are confident. Everything is going well.

2. From now on, you will not feel any vertigo. Every time you're near a high place, you will think that you feel just as good as when you (insert your pleasant experience). You are serene, happy, confident. You can go wherever you want. You are the master of your sensations.

Third step: ascending

Stagefright

We've all experienced stagefright in one form or another – before an exam, a competition, an interview or a public presentation. The feeling is harmless if it strikes us before the event but then disappears at the crucial moment of the event itself. However, in its more serious form stagefright does not disappear at the crucial moment, but actually becomes stronger, to the point where a person can lose control of his or her physical and intellectual faculties.

If you suffer from a serious form of stagefright, it's mainly because you lack self-confidence. Fortunately there is a multi-stage programme that can cure you. But you must stick to it!

1. Start to relax long before the event
A few weeks before the event in question, embark on a programme of relaxation. Any one of the methods described in this book can help you. Choose the one you like best.

2. Visualize success
Do regular visualization exercises in which the central theme is success. You will have no trouble using your imagination to create scenes in which you are applauded, praised, celebrated, congratulated, acclaimed and so on. The aim of these visualizations is to impress your subconscious with a sense of success.

3. Your self-hypnotic conditioning programme
Record a self-hypnotic programme, as you've already learnt to do. Start on the programme as soon as possible, in order to increase its

effectiveness. The example below is designed for passing an exam, but you can easily adapt it to any situation that might provoke stagefright.

Start recalling an experience that's pleasant, and that elicits feelings of peace and serenity.

ANTI-STAGEFRIGHT CONDITIONING

First step: descending

Second step

1. Give your stagefright an identifiable form. Look at it, see how mediocre and unimportant it is. It can't touch you, because your confidence is stronger than anything else. It is nothing compared to you. You are much stronger.
2. You know you can pass your exam, make your sales presentation or whatever. You know the material perfectly. You're ready. You have no reason to worry.
3. Your stagefright disappears little by little. It is conquered. You are stronger. You have confidence in yourself and in your abilities. You know you'll succeed. You are the stronger one.
4. From now on you will not experience any stagefright. You have defeated it once and for all. You are confident, and you're aware of your strengths. You are completely relaxed, peaceful, serene, just like the day when you (insert your positive experience). In future, whenever you have to take an exam, you will feel as good as the day you (insert your positive experience).

Third step: ascending

If you stick to this programme you should get rid of your stagefright in a few weeks. But don't think that this means you can neglect preparing for your exam or interview!

Concrete Phobias

When suffering from concrete phobias avoid doing *conscious* visualization exercises. These might have a traumatic effect on your subconscious, especially at the beginning of the programme.

As usual, frame the middle section (second step) of your conditioning, designed to combat your specific type of phobia, with the descending and ascending phases of the self-hypnotic method.

Animals

First step: descending

Second step

1. Close by you see a (cat, mouse, snake, spider, grasshopper etc.). You look at it and admire its beauty. You stare it in the eyes, remaining very calm and completely relaxed. You admire the way it's formed, the way it moves, its unique characteristics like speed or the noise it makes.
2. You stretch out your hand to touch it. The animal stays quiet. It seems to like your presence. It's happy to communicate with you. You are also happy to be with it. You touch it, and both you and the animal remain calm.

Third step: ascending

Plants

First step: descending

Second step

1. In front of you, you see (type of plant). Admire it. Look at the shape of its leaves, and the particular shades of green it has. Admire the form of its branches. See how beautiful its flowers are, how full and beautifully coloured. You are calm. You know that this (type of plant) cannot harm you in anyway. You are much stronger than it is. Look at it with affection. It seems to bloom under your gaze.
2. From now on, you will no longer be afraid of (type of plant). You know you are much stronger than it is. You consider it as a friend. Plants are beautiful, and enjoy the sunshine just like you do. We live together with plants on our beautiful planet.

Third step: ascending

Fear of the Dark

First step: descending

Second step

1. Dark is no different from light. Darkened rooms contain exactly the same things as they do during the day. Darkness comes so that everyone can rest quietly. Darkness helps you sleep. It gives you a rest from the light of day. We need darkness.
2. From now on you will have no fear of the dark. Nothing changes when it gets dark. There's no reason to be afraid. On the contrary, you know now that darkness is your friend, because it helps you rest.

Third step: ascending

Fear of Water

To increase the effectiveness of your conditioning, insert an experience from your past that was very positive and serene, and that has remained impressed on your memory.

First step: descending

Second step

1. You're at the summit of a mountain. You see a large lake below. You descend the mountain to get closer to it. There's a beautiful sandy beach around the lake.
2. You jump into the lake, smiling and happy. You're in the water because it gives you pleasure. No one is making you go any further. If you like, you can get out right away and return to the top of the mountain. You feel as calm and relaxed as the day you (insert positive experience).
3. From now on you will not be afraid of water. You know you have nothing to fear from it, that it's just an element of nature. You feel confident and happy in the water.

Third step: ascending

Free Yourself from Bad Habits – Tobacco, Alcohol, Drugs and Sweets

Any inveterate smoker or drinker, sugar junkie or drug addict knows about the devastating effects these deplorable habits have on the human body.

So why do people continue, if they know how bad their habit is? Because a habit of this kind, as well as being a physical dependency which is not always easy to break, is adopted not by the conscious mind but by the subconscious. So a conscious awareness of the harmful effects of tobacco, or a glance at the scales after an orgy of uncontrolled eating, are not very effective dissuading factors. You have to work on the subconscious level in order to free yourself of these habits and take control of your life.

Smoking

The harmful effects of smoking, both short- and long-term, are well known and don't need reiteration here. There are two methods available to those who want to give it up: one programme consists mainly of visualization exercises, while the other involves hypnotic conditioning.

THE 'AWAKENING' METHOD

Every day for a week do the following exercise, which aims to make your subconscious aware of your intention to give up smoking.

Preparatory exercise

Look through your photo albums for a picture of yourself before you started smoking, or, if you began as an adolescent, at least one from the time when you were less addicted. Try to find a picture in which you look happy and relaxed.

1. Retreat to your mental sanctuary and relax.
2. Visualize yourself as you were in the picture you found.
3. Now visualize yourself today, as you would be if you didn't smoke: you'd be in better physical shape, you'd have more endurance, you wouldn't be bothered by that persistent little irritating cough, you wouldn't spend the winter going from one cold to another. The air you'd breathe would always be purer, and your breath would smell a lot better. In short, you'd be in much better general health.
4. Do this exercise at least twice a week.

BLACKBOARD–WHITE BOARD EXERCISE

That's right, we're back to the old technique of the two boards – by now you should be an expert at it.

1. Retreat to your mental sanctuary.
2. On the blackboard, write the negative effects of smoking tobacco, for example:

    -   I cough in the morning when I wake up.
    -   I have bad breath.
    -   I'm always out of breath.
    -   I have no endurance.
    -   I suffer from cardiac problems.
    -   I catch one cold after another.
    -   I'm always tired. . . etc.

As usual, these sentences must be clearly legible on the blackboard. Impress them on your mind. Read them over a few times, and feel the anger growing inside you.

3. Now destroy the blackboard, venting all your rage. Remember, the

more violent your fury is, the more chance you have of getting rid of the tobacco habit.

4. Now calm yourself. Breathe deeply for a few moments. Visualize a pleasant scene, or look around your sanctuary, or think about someone you love.

Positive thoughts for giving up tobacco

1. When you've regained your serenity, turn to the white board and write the positive thoughts that would result from giving up smoking:

   - I don't cough any more.
   - My breath smells sweet.
   - I'm not out of breath.
   - I'm in great shape.
   - My heart is healthy and strong.
   - I can do sports . . . and so on.

2. Read these sentences over carefully a few times. Let the feeling of approval grow in you, and project it on to what you've written. Take your time and read over your positive thoughts again and again, thinking of all the benefits that stopping smoking will bring you.

3. Feel proud of your success, which you should consider as something already accomplished.

It's well worth the effort to persevere with this technique. Do it for at least two weeks, during which time your craving should diminish considerably. If you keep track of the number of cigarettes or cigars you smoke a day you will see the number dwindle, even without any conscious effort on your part.

It is possible that this little 'cure' will not free you of the habit completely, especially if you were a heavy smoker. If this is the case extend the exercise, using the twenty-one day method.

THE TWENTY-ONE-DAY METHOD

Before going to sleep, and just before getting up, do this:

1. Relax as fully as possible, using your favourite technique.
2. Retreat to your mental sanctuary, which now contains only the white board.

3. Write 'I don't smoke any more!' on the white board.
4. Then fall asleep, without letting the image of the blackboard enter your mind.
5. In the morning when you awaken, the first idea to enter your mind will be that you have conquered the smoking habit.
6. Do this little exercise for twenty-one days. If, after that time, you feel you have not entirely succeeded, strengthen your resolve by extending it to the three-month programme, which you're already familiar with.

HOW SELF-HYPNOSIS CAN HELP

Another plan of attack consists of using an appropriate self-hypnotic conditioning programme. In order to get rid of a deeply rooted habit like any kind of drug consumption, a real 'de-programming' plan is necessary. That is why the anti-smoking conditioning consists of the following stages:

1. Establishing the certainty of success.
2. Representing yourself as a fulfilled human being, full of energy and enthusiasm.
3. Developing in yourself feelings of disgust and distaste towards smoking.
4. Depicting yourself as a non-smoker.
5. Introducing new role models for your life, and new options and activities where smoking does not play a role.

Based on this plan, you can create your own conditioning. The important thing is that it adheres to the stages listed above.

Create Your Own Conditioning

The time it takes to effect a complete cure depends entirely on personal factors. How long have you been smoking? How many do you smoke per day? Where do you smoke? When do you smoke? Why?

The answers to the last three questions are of capital importance in developing your conditioning. So here's a list of probable responses. Tick off the ones which refer to you. In this way you can establish your smoking 'profile' so that you can use it when the time comes to tape your self-hypnotic conditioning. The programme to be outlined a little later will serve as a general model. To increase its effectiveness, you will then adapt it to your own personal needs.

Some people stop smoking right after the first session. Others have to stick to the programme for six months.

Finally, if you've already succeeded in stopping smoking for a few months or a few years, but you feel you might crack and resume the habit, don't hesitate to get back into your conditioning programme. The longer you put off the 'cure', the harder it will be to break the habit.

Here is a questionnaire which will establish your smoking 'profile'.

Your smoking profile

Where do you smoke?
- In the car
- On public transport
- At work
- Only in designated smoking areas
- At home
- In bars or restaurants
- Everywhere

When do you smoke?
- When you feel depressed
- When you're alone
- When you're bored
- When you're feeling under stress
- When you're with other smokers
- During or after meals
- All the time

Why do you smoke?
- To relax
- To fortify your courage
- To appear composed, calm and collected
- To help your digestion
- Because you live and/or work with other smokers
- Because you've been told smoking makes you eat less
- You feel the need without knowing why
- Other reasons

After filling in the questionnaire, write the alternative options which are possible for each heading. For example, if you smoke on public transport, your new option could be formulated as follows: 'Next time

I'll take a seat in the non-smoking section so that I won't be tempted to smoke.' If you smoke to relax, you can formulate your alternative as: 'The next time I need to relax, I'll do some breathing exercises and drink a glass of water or juice instead of lighting a cigarette. . .' and so on. Choose simple options which are accessible and easy to apply.

Now it's time to switch on your tape recorder and record the self-hypnotic conditioning messages that will form part of your 'de-programming'.

ANTI-SMOKING CONDITIONING

First step: descending

Second step

1. Relax. Think of all you've accomplished in your life, of all your past successes, all your positive actions. You are proud of yourself. Be proud of your intelligence, of your endurance at work, of your creativity. You're very satisfied with yourself.
2. You know you will continue to succeed, as you have up to now. You are more determined than ever to get rid of any obstacles that might hinder your progress, or anything unhealthy in your life.
3. You reject smoking because you know it is harming you. You do it for yourself, for your health and your wellbeing. And since your life has been a success, it will continue to be a success without smoking. You choose to be a non-smoker.
4. You can see yourself freed of the cigarette habit. You imagine yourself as a non-smoker. You give up tobacco and reject the destructive habit. Your body rejects it, your mind rejects it. You don't smoke, and you feel great.
5. Imagine that you're crushing a cigarette between your fingers. Imagine that you're throwing a pack of cigarettes out of the window. You feel great. Your decision is made. Your body rejects tobacco. Your lungs refuse to be poisoned, your heart beats more strongly, you have more breath, you can do your favourite sports without getting tired out. You're in perfect health.
6. The air around you is fresh and clean. That's what you want. Cigarettes disgust you. Your breath is fresh because you don't have the taste of cigarettes in your mouth. Your taste buds are much more sensitive, and you appreciate all the wonderful food you eat.

You've chosen to be healthy and strong, and your lungs are clean and full of pure air.

7. You have decided to live as pleasant a life as possible by becoming a non-smoker. You have deliberately chosen not to smoke, and you feel really good. You've found the way to get rid of your bad habits. (At this point, insert the new options which you've formulated according to your personal profile, using the same pronoun – you or I – that you've been using for the rest of the conditioning.)

8. Imagine your daily life (insert the times you tend to smoke during the course of an ordinary day) without cigarettes. No matter what the situation, you're a non-smoker. You love the pure air you breathe, and the health you enjoy. Continue imagining yourself living without tobacco for the entire day, happy to be a non-smoker. You feel marvellously well.

9. Your breathing gets better and better and you have more and more energy. You feel great. You have a lot of endurance. People you know are happy that you've successfully beaten the habit. You feel marvellously well without cigarettes. You are a non-smoker!

Third step: ascending

A FEW TRICKS TO MAKE BEATING THAT TOBACCO HABIT EASIER

Since you are determined to stop smoking, you might as well get all the odds in your favour. Here are a few very simple ideas which can make the task easier.

– set a precise date for beginning your programme, and a precise deadline for stopping smoking completely.
– Once you've decided to stop smoking, don't buy your preferred brand any more. Rather, buy a brand that you don't like.
– In the morning when you leave for work, leave your lighter or matches at home. You'll always have to ask someone for a light.
– After lighting a cigarette, try to smoke only half of it.
– On public transport, use your willpower to pick a seat in a non-smoking section.

Alcohol

The boundary between the casual drinker (someone who has a glass of alcohol from time to time) and the alcoholic is relatively vague. It gets even more difficult to define in the light of research which has shown it's possible to be alcoholic without ever giving the impression of drinking too much.

These days, a person with alcoholic tendencies is defined as someone who:

- feels the need to drink alcohol at certain times of the day
- drinks alone
- sometimes feels remorse or guilt after drinking alcohol
- is subject to mood changes due to alcohol consumption
- exhibits disproportionate anxiety when deprived of alcohol, for one reason or another.

If you fall into one of these categories, it's really time to do something about it. But to undertake a personal anti-alcohol programme you must first be very determined to succeed. You must make a firm resolve to get yourself out of the situation.

The stages you will follow are very similar to the anti-smoking programme. You have two possibilities: visualization exercises or self-hypnotic 'de-programming'.

But be warned that if you're already a severe alcoholic, you might need outside help. Your desire to stop drinking might not be enough. That doesn't mean to say that you shouldn't start on the personal programme described below – you just might have to complement your personal programme with visits to a therapist.

PERSONAL PROGRAMME TO GIVE UP ALCOHOL

1. Get comfortable in your mental sanctuary.
2. On the blackboard, write the negative effects resulting from your consumption of alcohol, for example:

   - alcohol makes me moody and short-tempered
   - alcohol is bad for my health
   - alcohol makes me fat
   - alcohol makes me look older than I am
   - alcohol has made me lose some friends
   - alcohol gives me bad breath

- alcohol is endangering my professional career
- when I drink, I'm ashamed of myself . . . and so on.

3. Read these messages over a few times before picking up your hammer and violently destroying the blackboard.
4. Calm down, take a few deep breaths, look around your sanctuary and try to recall a pleasant experience.
5. Once you're calm again, turn to the white board.
6. Write down the positive effects of not drinking:

- without alcohol I perform better at work
- when I don't drink I'm in better health
- when I don't drink I don't gain weight
- when I don't drink I'm not moody
- I look better when I don't drink . . . and so on.

7. Next, step back and read these messages over attentively, feeling a sense of self-approval. Let the beneficial feeling that these thoughts inspire fill your mind.
8. Imagine your new personality without alcohol. See yourself as you are, without the influence of alcohol to alter your character. Imagine how others react to you, how your friends will behave towards you, laugh with you, how your loved ones will treat you with affection and your colleagues with respect.

THE TWENTY-ONE-DAY PROGRAMME

If you feel these exercises aren't enough, try the twenty-one-day programme.

1. At night before going to sleep, visualize the white board and read over the messages which proclaim your victory over alcohol (sentences describing the positive effects of not drinking). Under no circumstances should the blackboard enter your mind.
2. Next day, the first image that enters your mind will be the white board.
3. Persevere for twenty-one days. If you need still more reinforcement, use the three-month programme: after twenty-one days take a week's break before beginning another twenty-one-day cycle, and continue this schedule for three months.

Important note

Remember that you cannot spread your subconscious around. It's useless to ask it to concentrate on more than one thing at a time. So if you feel you're not entirely successful in your efforts, think whether, in the course of the three months, you haven't used (or wanted to use) the blackboard–white board method for other purposes.

SELF-HYPNOSIS WILL HELP

You can undertake a self-hypnotic 'de-programming' cure by following the steps outlined in the section on tobacco. When you have established your drinking 'profile' with the help of the questionnaire below, use it to adapt your hypnotic de-programming to your own personal situation.

It is possible that you'll stop drinking in just a few days, especially if you're not a confirmed alcoholic. If you're more deeply involved with alcohol, it might take a few weeks. Don't get discouraged, the mere act of trying proves that you're on the right road.

Your drinking profile

Where do you drink?
– When you get together with other people
– In bars and/or restaurants
– At home
– In planes, or at the airport before a flight
– At your office
– In hiding
– All of the above
– Other places

When do you drink?
– Only at night
– At all hours of the day
– During meals
– Before meals
– Before taking a plane
– With friends who drink
– When you're alone

Why do you drink?
- To relax
- To forget your troubles
- Because you like the taste of alcohol
- Because you feel more grown up or mature
- Because it gives you an excuse to act in an irresponsible way
- To imitate your friends and/or relatives
- To stimulate yourself
- To fight insomnia
- Because your life seems boring

How to proceed

After checking off the responses which apply to your case, write down your new options. For example, if you drink alcohol before meals you might choose to replace it with fruit juice. If you drink because you find life boring, you could formulate your new option like this: 'Whenever I feel this deep-seated sense of boredom with my life, I'll call one of my friends. . .'.

When you've finished listing your options you're ready to record your self-hypnotic conditioning, which should be planned according to a well-defined progression.

1. Condition yourself to be confident of your success.
2. Condition yourself to find alcohol disgusting.
3. Create a sensible and healthy image of yourself.
4. Represent yourself as a 'sober' person.
5. Provide yourself with the new options which you have formulated according to your 'drinking profile'.

ANTI-ALCOHOL CONDITIONING

First step: descending

Second step

1. Relax and think of all your accomplishments, all the good things you've done in your life, all the love you've given and received. Feel proud of your intelligence and your perseverance. Feel proud to be who you are.

2. Because you've done so much with your life, you are firmly

motivated to reject any habit that is harmful to you. You reject alcohol. You are right not to drink. You feel marvellously well. You do not drink alcohol. You feel good. You will continue feeling good because you don't drink alcohol.

3. Imagine yourself as a non-drinker. You are sober and clear-headed, and you like that. You reject alcohol. Your body rejects it, and your mind rejects it.

4. Imagine yourself destroying a bottle of alcohol, or emptying a bottle of alcohol into the sink. You feel good. The act of destroying the alcohol gives you pleasure. You've made the choice to stop drinking, and all is well. Your body doesn't desire alcohol: your liver, your kidneys, your arteries and your heart do not want any more alcohol. They want to be healthy and strong again.

5. Alcohol disgusts you. Your breath is fresh, sweet-smelling. You don't have to chew mints to hide from people around you the fact that you've been drinking. You enjoy eating again. You feel good. You look good. You are a non-drinker.

6. You've chosen to be a non-drinker. You choose not to drink the next glass of alcohol, and you're satisfied with that choice. You do not drink alcohol.

7. Imagine your daily life without alcohol. You're happy. You carry out your daily activities without drinking alcohol. You have chosen instead to (insert your new options, using the same personal pronoun – you or I – as you've been using up to now).

8. You are succeeding. You do not drink alcohol, and everything's going well in your life. Imagine your daily life without alcohol. Every day you (insert a daily activity) without drinking alcohol. You feel calm, relaxed, happy and proud not to be drinking.

9. You are sober. You do not drink alcohol. Your life is a success. You are happy and serene.

Third step: ascending

You might find this conditioning programme slightly overstated and therefore difficult for your subconscious to accept. If so, when you tape your session replace the sentences that depict your cure as a *fait accompli* with less explicit ones, leaving some room for nuance. For example, 'You do not drink alcohol. . .' can be replaced by 'You drink less alcohol than you did last week. . .'. Continue reducing the amount until you are ready for a total affirmation: 'You do not drink alcohol at all.'

Helpful hints

- Don't keep a store of your favourite drink in the house.
- When you're in a restaurant or bar, choose an alcoholic drink that you don't like.
- Calculate the amount of money you will save each year by not drinking.
- Avoid stressful situations as much as possible during your cure. For example, don't choose a time of year when you know you'll be over-loaded with work, or when you'll be studying for exams.
- Enlist the help of your partner or a close friend. Review your eating habits, and refer to a good book on nutrition to help you plan a healthy diet, rich in vitamins and minerals.
- If you're in the habit of drinking a few glasses of wine with your meals, stop salting your food – then you'll be less thirsty when you eat. Also try to avoid spicy foods during your cure, for the same reason.

Clean Out Your Medicine Cabinet

The abuse of medication is one of the negative habits that char-acterizes our society. Factories producing pharmaceutical products are among the richest businesses on the planet. We all know people who get angry when a doctor refuses to prescribe them medication for their slightest ailment.

We take medication to get rid of symptoms that we could eliminate just as easily by reshaping our lifestyle. Worse still, we unknowingly absorb a host of chemical products with incompatible effects which play havoc with our poor bodies. So what can you do if you are a slave to medication?

A QUESTION OF LIFESTYLE

Obviously the first thing you have to do is examine your lifestyle. Let's look at a concrete example.

Imagine that for years now you've been taking a laxative every night, as millions of people do. You are convinced that your intestines are too 'lazy' and can't function without it. You've already tried cutting down the dosage, but to no avail. What can you do?

First, examine your diet. Are you drinking at least two pints of water a day? Are you eating enough fruit and raw vegetables?

Next, take a look at the way you live. Lazy bowels result from a sedentary lifestyle. Do you walk enough? Do you climb stairs or take the lift? Do you do any sports? If not, stir things up a little. You'll soon notice a marked difference.

So whether you're taking medication to stimulate or to slow down your bowels, or to ease pains caused by headaches or rheumatism, or to sleep better or digest your food better, the first thing to do is carefully examine your lifestyle. That's where you're most likely to find the root of your disorder.

USE THE FOUNTAIN OF YOUTH CURE

Do you remember the fountain of youth, which can help prevent ageing? It can also be used to get rid of a dependence on medication.

Fountain of health exercise

Do this exercise at least once a day.

1. Get comfortable in your mental sanctuary.
2. Construct your own fountain of health. If you already have a fountain of youth, you can use it as your fountain of health.
3. When you've visualized the fountain in detail, as you've already learnt to do, approach it calmly.
4. Get undressed and dive in. Enjoy the sensation of the purifying water. Feel the freshness in your body. Tell yourself that the water is cleansing you of all your minor ailments. Tell yourself you feel fine, and that you don't need your medication. You feel good, and the water makes you feel happy.
5. Now come out of the fountain. You are free of your dependency on medication, you're in great shape. All your bodily functions are in perfect order. You are happy and free. You look fantastic.
6. Immerse yourself in the fountain as often as you like. Each time see yourself cured of all your minor ailments, and liberated from your stock of pills.

USE EVERYTHING YOU'VE LEARNT UP TO NOW

Once you've resolved to improve your lifestyle, and you've overcome your tendency to resort to medication by applying the fountain of youth exercise, get into the habit of solving any problems that might arise and of easing any discomfort you might experience by applying the techniques presented in this book. Re-read Chapters 11 and 12 and apply the methods described in them. If you put your mind to it, and do your part, you will notice an improvement in just a few days.

STRESS MUST BE ELIMINATED FROM YOUR LIFE

You will be aware that stress is a major cause of common disorders. You may eat excellent food, do lots of sports, love your work and have a happy personal life . . . but if your life still contains elements of stress, then the symptoms which caused you to turn to medication in the first place will not be long in recurring. So one of the best things you can do to be happy is to eliminate the curse of stress by following the method described in Chapter 11. If you haven't already started using it, it's high time you did. Refresh your memory, and embark on a full-scale war to eliminate this horrible monster which can devour your health and sanity.

Drugs

Once again it is unnecessary to restate the negative effects that drugs have on our health and personality. What is important, when undertaking a personal 'detox' programme, is to be firmly resolved to see it through.

The techniques of psychocybernetics, based mainly on visualization, are undoubtedly effective. However, considering the extreme influence that drugs can have on the brain and the human body, some sort of complementary treatment is usually necessary. If you consult a hypnotherapist to help you break your drug habit, it is probable that he or she will recommend a personal psychocybernetic programme to complement the treatment. You will therefore feel, and justifiably so, that you are actively participating in your own cure by using your own initiative to reinforce results obtained through the therapy programme.

Self-hypnosis is not a recommended treatment for curing a highly destructive habit like drug addiction. It seems that these drugs, whatever category they fall into (stimulants, tranquillizers, hallucinogens etc.), influence cerebral chemistry in such a way that any attempts at self-hypnosis become either dangerous or completely useless. Therefore, as far as hypnosis goes, leave the deconditioning work to your therapist.

Now let's look at what you can do to help yourself. The programme consists of three important exercises and you should start by setting aside a quiet time of day for them.

PREPARATORY EXERCISE

1. If you've been taking drugs for some time, you've probably noticed some physical deterioration. Look for a photograph of yourself which was taken before you started taking drugs. If you've been on the drugs since adolescence, find a photograph in which you still look healthy and happy.
2. Get comfortable in a room where you won't be disturbed.
3. Study the photograph carefully. Impress it on your mind in as much detail as possible.
4. If you already have created a mental sanctuary, use it now.
5. Visualize yourself as you were in the photograph. You look healthy and happy. Your whole life lies ahead of you. Your friends like you, your family loves you, your colleagues respect you.
6. Savour this ideal image of yourself for a few moments. Feel the happiness you experienced at that time. Tell yourself you want to be like that again.
7. Open your eyes and breathe deeply.

ANTI-DRUG PROGRAMME

Once again we turn to our friends, the black and white boards.

1. Retreat to your mental sanctuary.
2. Try to relax completely by applying one of the methods in this book.
3. Approach the blackboard with a piece of chalk in your hand.
4. Write down all the negative aspects of taking drugs, for example:

   • Drugs destroy my health.
   • Drugs make me lose the affection of my loved ones.
   • Drugs compromise my professional career.

- I am ashamed of taking drugs . . . and so on.

If you really want to get rid of your problem, you will have no trouble finding things to write on the blackboard.

5. Read your thoughts over. Feel the anger growing inside you, until it becomes too violent to contain.
6. Now destroy the blackboard, channelling all your hate and disgust. The more violent you are, the more likely you'll be to get through to your subconscious.
7. Now calm yourself. Do a few breathing exercises. Think of someone you love, or visualize a pleasant memory.
8. Turn to the white board. Write down everything positive that will result from your giving up drugs. For example:

- Without drugs I'll work better.
- Without drugs my health will improve.
- People will respect me if I stop taking drugs.
- I'm proud of myself and my success.

9. Read over these positive thoughts while experiencing feelings of joy and approval. Let these positive feelings fill you completely.

THE THREE-MONTH METHOD

You'll probably have to reinforce the effects of the above exercise with the three-month method. So do the exercise every day for twenty-one days, then rest for a week, after which you start again for another twenty-one-day cycle, and so on for three months.

Once again, remember that the subconscious is incapable of dealing with more than one problem at a time. So you must at all costs avoid trying to work on another problem during the three-month period.

THE LIBERATING FOUNTAIN

Why not combine the preceding exercises with the fountain of health technique? In this way you will reinforce the positive self image which you have created by conditioning your subconscious.

1. As usual, retreat to your mental sanctuary.
2. If you have not already done so, build a fountain. If you already have a fountain of youth, use it as your fountain of health.
3. Dive into the fountain. Feel the fresh, purifying water on your body. Take pleasure in the marvellous sensations which pervade

your entire body, while you wash away all the negative aspects of your old behaviour patterns.

4. Emerge from the water feeling purified and in excellent health. Visualize yourself as healthy and rested, happy, in the best of moods, full of energy and feeling wonderful.
5. Dive back into the fountain a few times. Each time you come out, feel the renewed energy and health you have acquired.
6. Between each entry, breathe deeply the pure, calming air of your sanctuary.

The Demon Sugar

Producing the combined effect of unbalancing mineral salt content, causing allergic reactions, and partially suppressing white blood cells, sugar destroys the immune system and slowly but surely leads to degenerative disease.

Nancy Appleton, *Lick the Sugar Habit*

From childhood on we are programmed to consider sweets as a kind of 'reward', and being denied puddings as a punishment. Almost everyone likes sweet things to some degree.

Psychologists know perfectly well why some of us abuse sweets. A few minutes of conversation with a person is enough to reveal the origin of this addition – yes, addiction is exactly what it is! What can be done to moderate this lust for sugary things of all kinds?

The path you will follow closely resembles those used for tobacco and alcohol addiction, since this too is a question of a bad habit which has been impressed on your subconscious mind.

The most effective exercise you can do to get rid of your passion for sweets is, once again, the blackboard–white board technique.

EXERCISE FOR GIVING UP SUGAR SIMPLY AND EFFECTIVELY

1. As usual, retreat to your mental sanctuary and relax.
2. Pick up a piece of chalk and write your negative thoughts on the blackboard:

   - Sweets are bad for my health.
   - Sweets make me gain weight.
   - Sweets destroy my teeth.
   - Sweets cause pimples . . . and so on.

3. Then, after having read these messages over and over, and having let a feeling of disgust and rejection grow inside you, pick up your hammer and destroy the blackboard. Exteriorize all your hate through this action.
4. Calm yourself. Breathe deeply, relax, think about something pleasant.
5. Now write your positive thoughts on the white board:

   • Without sweets, my skin is fresh and pure.
   • Without sweets I don't gain weight.
   • Without sweets I don't run the risk of getting diabetes . . . and so on.

6. Read these positive messages over with a feeling of complete approval about yourself. Project an image of yourself that you like, as a person with the willpower to succeed.

Your self-hypnosis programme *will* work! There's no doubt you will succeed, as long as you are resolved to get rid of your bad habit. Now establish your sweet-eating 'profile'.

Your sweet-eating profile

Where do you eat sweets?
– At home
– In the car
– On public transport
– Other

When do you eat sweets?
– After meals
– At all hours of the day
– At night
– When you feel a little hungry
– When you're with others who eat too much
– When you're depressed
– When you're worried
– Other

Why do you eat sweets?
– For gratification
– Because you stopped smoking
– To break your daily routine

- To compensate for unpleasant occurrences
- Other

How to proceed

After checking off the cases which apply to you, write down your new options. For example, if you eat sweets to break your daily routine, your new option could read as follows: 'The next time I need a break in my routine, I'll call a friend or I'll write a letter. . .' and so on.

Now it's time to record your self-hypnosis programme, as you have been taught to do throughout this book. It should include the following elements:

- Instil a sense of self-confidence.
- Get you disgusted with sweets.
- Create a positive self image.
- Include the new options which you've developed with the help of your profile.

CONDITIONING AGAINST SUGAR ABUSE

First step: descending

Second step

1. You have relaxed by thinking about the positive things you've accomplished in your life. You have confidence in your potential, in your intelligence, in your creativity. You are proud of yourself. You have succeeded and you will continue to succeed. You are resolved to reject the bad habits which are causing you harm.
2. You now reject, once and for all, your tendency to eat too many sweets. You don't like sweets. You reject them because they're harmful to your body. They're harmful to your teeth. They make you fat. You don't like them. You find sweets disgusting.
3. Since you have succeeded in everything you've really wanted to do in the past, you will succeed again now and rid yourself of this bad habit. You don't eat sweets. They're bad for your health. You want to be healthy, in top shape, fit and trim, energetic.
4. Imagine how you are without eating sweets. Imagine yourself refusing to eat sweets that are offered to you. Imagine yourself being strong and perfectly capable of rejecting this bad habit. You

don't like sweets. You feel good and free. You choose not to indulge yourself by eating sweets.

5. You do not eat sweets. Imagine your life without sweets. Imagine that you are (insert one of your daily activities) without feeling the slightest need to eat sweets. You don't like sweets. But you do like your health. You're energetic and in top shape. You don't eat sweets.

From now on, you (here insert your new options, being careful to use the same pronoun you've used up to now). You feel fine. You are free of your bad habit. You feel calm and fit, because you don't eat sweets. You feel good about yourself. You look great in your clothes. You have good teeth and a beautiful skin because you don't eat sweets.

6. You have succeeded. You don't like sweets, and you're proud of yourself. You're very relaxed. You feel marvellous. You don't like sweets. Everything is fine.

Third step: ascending

Some hints to help you succeed

- It's obviously easier to get rid of your sweet tooth if you don't keep supplies in the house.
- Eat a good breakfast. This will prevent that eleven o'clock hunger attack.
- Keep something healthy to nibble on handy, like raw carrots or celery, some cold chicken, nuts and of course fruit.
- If it's too much for you to give up sweets all at once, you can munch on dried fruit from time to time (raisins, apricots, apples etc.).

The Ring-Stop Method for all Addictions

This technique has been successfully applied by a young psychologist, principally in eliminating tobacco addiction in his patients. However, it can be adapted for any kind of negative addiction.

The patricians of ancient Rome had a special trick which allowed them to decide if they'd had too much to drink or not. They had a sentence engraved in minuscule letters on one of their rings. When they became incapable of reading the tiny letters correctly, they knew they'd reached a sufficient degree of inebriation. The ring-stop technique is derived from this practice.

First buy yourself a ring (you don't have to spend a fortune, but you should like the ring enough to wear it). Wear it on your right or left hand, as you prefer.

Every day for a week get comfortable on a sofa and look at your ring for a few minutes, saying to yourself:

- This simple ring is the symbol of my new behaviour
- It will help me overcome my addiction
- It reprents health, joy, happiness, good humour, energy and enthusiasm
- It represents my victory over (your bad habit)
- It is my weapon against (your bad habit)

. . . And so on. Do this regularly and faithfully for about ten minutes at each sitting.

From then on, each time you pick up a cigarette or a glass of alcohol, a sweet, a tranquillizer etc., the ring will tell you to stop. It's as simple as that. It will become a red light in your mind, without your even having to think about it.

Do you think it's too simple? You have nothing to lose by trying, do you? The essential thing is to believe it can work. This technique has worked for others – why shouldn't it work for you too?

CHAPTER 15

How to Win the Weight War

Whether it's a question of gaining or losing weight, those odd pounds always seem to find a way of ruining our lives. What can be done to control the weight problem once and for all?

Getting your subconscious to work for you is essential both for trimming down when you're overweight and for building up when you're too thin. You have to replace that dumpy or skinny self image with a new one, the image you've always dreamed of having. You've probably been over- or under-weight for a long time. So this undesirable self image is deeply anchored in your subconscious. Therefore you'll have to be very persevering. What your sub-conscious has been 'seeing' over a period of years cannot be changed in a week. You'll need a few months of dedicated work.

Once again we must remind you that in order to succeed you have to concentrate your subconscious on only one goal at a time. If you start a programme of weight control, concentrate all your efforts on it and, until you've attained your goal, avoid making other demands of your subconscious.

What is interesting about the method that you're going to learn is that not only will you be able to trim down or firm up your figure, you'll also be able to work on certain specific parts of your body. For example, by following this programme you can build up or thin down your legs or your arms, take a few pounds off the stomach area, tailor your waist or your buttocks, fill out your breasts or hips and so on. But of course you must be firmly convinced of your eventual success.

First here are the methods that can be applied to both types of problems – losing and gaining weight.

Losing or Gaining – a Single State of Mind

Let's imagine that you're a few pounds overweight. You've tried a whole series of diets, some serious, some rather bizarre; you try to lead an active life; the battery of tests you've undergone show no hormonal imbalances. In short – you're desperate!

Another possible scenario: you want to put on a few pounds. But although you've been eating like a horse and sleeping long hours, you still haven't been able to fill out. The numerous medical examinations you've had show no hormonal imbalances, no trace of a hyperthyroid condition, no 'gnawing' disease. What to do?

Don't be discouraged: there are a number of options open to you. You just have to apply the techniques of visualization which you're already familiar with.

THE FOUNTAIN OF BEAUTY

Once again turn to your fountain of youth, which you will now use as a fountain of beauty.

1. Retreat to your mental sanctuary and approach your fountain.
2. When you dive in, see yourself as you are, either too fat or too thin. Feel the fresh water on your body, breathe in the pure air of your sanctuary.
3. Come out of the fountain. You now possess the figure of your dreams. You see yourself perfectly clearly, either thinned down or filled out, just as for years you wished you could look.
4. Dive back into the fountain a number of times. Each time you emerge, you see yourself as you've always wanted to be.
5. Feel the difference. Your body is supple. Where before you had folds of flab, your skin is now smooth and firm. Where your bones stuck out before, you find firm, soft flesh.
6. Love your new body. Tell your body how much you admire it. Allow a feeling of satisfaction to spread through you. Run, jump, dance, sing for joy in your mental sanctuary.

EXERCISE: THE IDEAL SELF-PORTRAIT

You can accompany your beauty baths with an exercise designed to improve your self image. It has two stages. The first can be done anywhere, any time. The second requires a few minutes of calm, since you will have to enter your mental sanctuary.

First step

1. Find a photograph of yourself in which you have the figure you'd like. If you've never had an ideal figure, find a photograph of yourself that you like and have it retouched. Or just cut a picture of an ideal figure out of a magazine and stick your head on it.
2. Study this image. Look at it attentively, concentrate all your visual energy on it. This image is you. You must become so familiar with it that you can reproduce it in your mind whenever you want.
3. Close your eyes and picture your new figure. Keep repeating that this is the real you. Do the exercise whenever you have a spare moment, at home or at work, on the bus or while waiting in a queue. Your subconscious will eventually get the message.

Second step

1. When you've got used to visualizing yourself at any time of day as you'd like to be, retreat to your mental sanctuary at least once a day.
2. Imagine that you're engaged in some activity you like, but which was prohibited by your previous physical condition. For example:

   - Practise some sport, proud of your supple, strong body, wearing a brightly coloured outfit.
   - Dressed in clothes that you've always wanted to wear but that you couldn't before, like tightly fitting slacks if you were too fat, or a low-cut dress or bathing suit if you were too bony. Just let your imagination go and you won't lack ideas.

3. Now imagine that your friends and family notice your new figure and make flattering comments about it. You can 'hear' their voices perfectly.

HOW TO IMPROVE CERTAIN PARTS OF YOUR BODY

As stated at the beginning of this chapter, these exercises can be used just as effectively to improve certain parts of your body as to work on your whole figure. You just have to adapt your visualization exercises accordingly.

In the fountain of beauty exercise, concentrate on changing the appearance of the parts of the body in question: legs, thighs, stomach, chest, waist etc. In the self-portrait exercise, find a photograph in which the central figure (you or a composite) possesses the characteristics which you would like to have.

That's all there is to it!

WHEN IT'S A QUESTION OF OVEREATING

It's one thing faithfully to practise the exercises described above, but if, as the heading suggests, your problem is due to overeating (whatever kind of food you abuse) then not only are you harming your figure, but you're destroying your health as well. Therefore, it might be a good idea to start modifying your diet.

If your weight problem is due solely to an excessive intake of sugar, then you already know what to do about it. Turn to Chapter 14, which explains how to rid yourself of this harmful habit.

It's also possible that you're eating foods which are too high in calories, or simply that your meals are unbalanced. The methods suggested here will allow you to review your calorie intake without suffering any of the psychological and physiological problems associated with all diets: depression, mood changes, insomnia, dreams about food, sensitivity to cold, migraines, apathy and so on. You will be able to generate in your subconscious feelings of disgust for all harmful substances, while at the same time creating an appetite for healthy foods. You will therefore experience none of the unpleasant frustrations generally associated with adhering to a strict diet.

BLACKBOARD–WHITE BOARD EXERCISE

1. Retreat to your mental sanctuary and pick up the white chalk.
2. On the blackboard, write the names of all the foods that you should avoid completely, or that you should eat only very infrequently. Don't just write things like 'fat foods' or 'sweets'. Specify exactly which foods you should abstain from, for example butter, chips, crisps, sausages, cakes, ice cream, chocolate, biscuits etc. If you have certain weaknesses for unwholesome foods, mention them specifically. Don't be ashamed of your weaknesses. You can always tell yourself that you'll be the only one to see your blackboard.

3. Read through your list with a feeling of disgust for these harmful foods. You're fed up with them. You hate them because they are destroying your health.
4. Now destroy the blackboard, channelling all your hate and disgust into the act.
5. Calm down, and relax for a few moments.
6. Now write down on the white board all the foods that you should eat to replace those which you want to eliminate: fresh fruit, vegetables, boiled or baked potatoes, lean meat, yoghurt, skimmed milk, low fat cheeses, etc.
7. Read through the white board's list a few times, with a sense of approval. You can feel your mouth salivate in anticipation as you read the names of these healthy foods which have become your new friends.

THE TWENTY-ONE-DAY METHOD

Use the twenty-one-day method to change your eating habits. If you feel twenty-one days is not sufficient, use the three-month cycle.

Be patient. Your bad eating habits are deeply embedded in your subconscious and exercise a firm control over your taste buds. Changing your tastes will take time. If you persevere, you will be satisfied with the results. By changing your eating habits and losing weight you will not only acquire your ideal figure, you'll also strengthen your system against illness. And as a bonus, you'll live longer.

BE REALISTIC IN YOUR HOPES

The more realistic you are, the more likely you'll be to attain your goals. Therefore, before saying 'I want to lose weight' or 'I want to put on weight', consult a table that lists the ideal weight in relation to your height and bone structure. Every doctor has one, and you can also find them in the chemist's and books on diet and nutrition. Organizations like Weight Watchers publish them regularly.

Consulting the chart will help you set your objectives. Don't forget – the subconscious likes precision.

WHAT IF YOU'RE NEITHER TOO FAT NOR TOO THIN?

It might be possible that, taking into account your bone structure, height and sex, you fall into an ideal weight range, despite what you think. It's also possible that your figure may be perfectly normal in the eyes of a doctor, but doesn't fit the current trend in fashions, which gives you the impression that something's wrong with it. If so, specify which part of your body bothers you, and base your programme of weight modification on improving it.

It is, however, more difficult to gain or lose weight when you fall into an 'ideal' zone, as specified on nutrition charts. Your body feels good with that weight, so your subconscious will have all the more work to do to change it. But be patient and persevere.

WHAT IF YOU HAVE A LOT OF WEIGHT TO LOSE OR GAIN?

In this case, the best solution is to proceed gradually. Don't start your exercise thinking that you'll be able to drop 15 lbs all at once. Don't traumatize your subconscious by asking the impossible.

Think in terms of stages of 5 lbs, for example. As already explained, it'll probably take a few months to attain your final objective. But above all, be confident.

THE BENEFITS OF EXERCISE

As you gradually get thinner or heavier, you will no doubt be tempted to consolidate your efforts through an exercise programme, since you will have a lot more energy to dispose of. Nothing could be better! But to avoid accident or injury be sure to ask the advice of a competent professional, especially if you haven't done any sports for a long time.

Also remember that muscles weigh more than fat. Therefore, as you gradually replace fat with muscle you might see your weight go up instead of down. Don't worry about it, and calmly continue with your programme.

Exercise does not cause spectacular weight loss in slightly overweight individuals. It strengthens and firms up the body, gets rid of those unsightly folds of flab, and balances out the figure. It can also reduce your appetite, if done rigorously and before meals. On the other hand, exercise can easily fill out persons who are too thin by making them 'grow' a covering of muscle over their bones.

Therefore, whether you're too fat or too thin, it's probable that if you undertake a programme of regular exercise you'll gain a little weight in the process.

How to Combat Cellulite

As you probably know, cellulite is a different kind of problem from simply being fat. You must have met people who, despite having a very slim figure, still have that 'orange peel' skin on the sides or backs of their thighs.

Cellulite occurs because of a thickening of the subcutaneous tissue, especially in women. Men do get cellulite, but it is rare. Diets cannot cure cellulite, which has absolutely nothing to do with calorie intake. Exercise can, to some extent, replace cellulite tissue with muscle tissue. Cycling is expecially effective in breaking up cellulite on the upper thighs. It has also been discovered that certain products have a tendency to 'stabilize' the condition. If you smoke and drink a lot of coffee, for example, your cellulite may become resistant to all forms of treatment.

Bathe in your fountain of beauty

One of the best mental techniques that you can use to eliminate or at least reduce your cellulite is the fountain of beauty. When you emerge from your fountain, imagine that the areas where you have cellulite are firm and smooth, free of the unsightly swelling that characterizes the condition. Concentrate all your visualization efforts on those specific parts of the body.

Exercise to sculpt your figure

Now you're going to play artist with your own body.

1. Get comfortable in your mental retreat.
2. Visualize yourself as you are with your areas of 'orange peel' skin.
3. Now imagine that you're a clay statue.
4. Take a sculptor's chisel. Hold it firmly in your hand and start to chip away at your cellulite. Work slowly and calmly. Don't get agitated. You feel a great sense of satisfaction from the work you're doing.
5. When you've finished, put down the chisel, step back and admire your masterpiece.
6. Be proud of yourself. Allow a deep feeling of approval to flow through you.

Cellulite does not appear from one day to the next. It will therefore not disappear instantaneously, either. Be patient and persevere. Combine the two exercises every day. You should get results in a few months. In the meantime, there's nothing to stop you from taking concrete measures to accelerate your victory, and above all to consolidate it once it's achieved.

Change your lifestyle

If you smoke, or if you drink a lot of coffee, the desire to eliminate cellulite can serve as an added motivational factor in giving up these harmful habits. Follow the instructions in Chapter 14 for eliminating addiction to certain harmful substances.

To get rid of an exaggerated need for coffee, follow the instructions for eliminating sugar dependency. Warning: don't stop drinking coffee altogether from one day to the next. If you do you'll get headaches. Reduce your consumption to three cups per day (with no cream or sugar if possible) and stick to this limit.

If your work is sedentary, your cellulite is probably concentrated in the upper thighs. Therefore, try to spend as little time as possible sitting down. Use any excuse to get up and activate your thigh muscles.

Fight stress

In some people, stress accentuates water retention in the body. You might be mistaking what you think is cellulite for tissue that is retaining too much water.

If so, go back and study the section on stress (pp. 84–6). Fight against the psychological tensions in your life. You will soon eliminate water retention as well.

CHAPTER 16

Insomnia – How to Eliminate It Once and for All

Insomnia is a modern problem. It affects millions of people, three-quarters of whom resort to a battery of sleeping pills, tranquillizers and other drugs for a solution. Some people have trouble getting to sleep before two or three o'clock in the morning, while others fall asleep at a normal hour but suddenly find themselves wide awake in the middle of the night. Why?

Eleven Simple Causes of Insomnia

Before discussing the psychological causes, let us remember that insomnia can result from material and physical causes which are easy to overcome with a bit of good old common sense instead of becoming a slave to medication.

- Do you have a good-quality, firm mattress?
- Is the temperature in your bedroom right? (The ideal sleeping temperature is somewhere between 17 and 20°C – about 65°F.)
- If you wear nightclothes, are they too tight?
- Are you in the habit of eating a heavy meal before going to bed?
- Do you make the mistake of doing strenuous exercise a couple of hours or so before going to bed?
- Does too much light come through your bedroom window?
- Are you really tired (physically) when you go to sleep?
- Are you, conversely, too tired when you go to sleep?

- If you share your bed with someone, do they move around too much during the night?
- Are your bedclothes made of a material that is irritating to your skin? For example, certain synthetic fabrics contain particles suspected of causing hyperactivity.
- Is your pillow too hard, too soft, or too high?

Finally, after answering the above questions, here's a very simple suggestion: have you tried placing your bed in a north–south direction, which corresponds to the magnetic field of the earth? You may notice an improvement.

Examine Yourself

Despite this long list, the most frequent causes of insomnia are psychological. We sleep badly because we're anxious or worried. We bring our cares to bed with us instead of leaving them at the bedroom door. Obviously a vicious circle soon establishes itself: you sleep badly because you're anxious about something, and the more you lack sleep the more anxious you get. Eventually, just the thought of lying in bed for hours, unable to fall asleep, listening to the walls creak, becomes an obsession and in itself prevents you from sleeping. So you will have to learn to clean up your act as far as your anxieties are concerned.

If you've had insomnia for a long time, and are in the habit of taking sleeping pills or tranquillizers, you first have to stop taking them. Go back and read the chapter on bad habits (Chapter 14) to learn how to free yourself of your dependence on medication. It is essential that you resolve to do this. Sleeping pills destroy your health, you can be sure of that.

The Secret of Sleeping Well

To sleep well, you have to know how to relax. If you can't relax spontaneously, learn how to do it consciously. Use one of the relaxation methods described in Part One of this book. Every night when you go to bed (which should be at approximately the same hour) relax by doing the exercise you've chosen. When you think you're relaxed enough, retreat to your mental sanctuary for a few visualization exercises. Do you remember the 'geyser' and the 'flexing' exercises (pp. 95

and 40), which were designed to help calm people down who are always on edge? Well, they're also very effective for relaxing before sleep. The geyser exercise will help you get rid of all the mental toxins you've accumulated during the day, while the flexing exercise will have a calming effect on your body itself.

These two exercises complement each other extremely well, and are very effective in inducing sleep. So make use of them each night.

EXERCISE TO PREPARE FOR SLEEP

While relaxing in your mental sanctuary, try to imagine yourself taking a walk somewhere that you like. For example:

1. You're walking along a beach of fine sand. It stretches away out of sight. There's the calm, crystalline, turquoise ocean on one side, and beautiful white chalk cliffs on the other. You can see the triangular sails of boats on the horizon.
2. You walk calmly along the beach, looking in front of you. Then you turn towards the cliffs and notice a narrow path, which you start climbing.
3. You emerge on to a meadow of fresh green grass, dotted with flowers. In the distance you see the tower of a village church, visible through the summer haze. Everything is calm, you feel the cool grass underfoot. The sea shimmers down below. You sit in the grass at the edge of the cliff and look out over the sea. The sun goes down slowly, and finally sets on the horizon.
4. Darkness grows softly around you. Little by little you feel yourself growing tired. You stretch out in the grass to look up at the stars, which appear one by one. The sky gets darker. It's night. You close your eyes. . . .

Of course you can create your own scene. It should, however, contain three elements:

- It should be a peaceful, quiet scene.
- It ends with night falling.
- You always finish by closing your eyes.

Self-hypnosis and Sleep

Hypnosis can do a lot to help you. If your insomnia is caused by anxiety, worries, fear of the future or obsessive thinking about current problems, you can eliminate the cause with a few self-hypnosis sessions. Get out your tape machine and record the following programmes, which you will listen to when you go to bed. Try to use a machine that turns itself off automatically, because you'll probably be asleep before the end of the tape.

THE MORPHEUS TECHNIQUE

First step: descending

Second step

1. You fall asleep easily. You love your sleep. Every night when you go to bed, you forget about your worries, your anxieties, your fears. You feel a wonderful sense of peace growing inside you. You are happy, relaxed, calm, ready for a good night's sleep.
2. You do not wake up during the night. Everything is fine. Everything is quiet. You sleep deeply right through to the morning. You are calm, and you don't think about anything. You just sleep. You sleep deeply.
3. Everything around you is calm. You do not wake up. You sleep deeply. You are relaxed and happy. Everything is fine.
4. When you awaken in the morning you will be full of energy, refreshed from your wonderful sleep. You'll be ready to do a thousand and one things, because you will have enjoyed a wonderful sleep. You'll be in a good mood, full of enthusiasm. Every night you will sleep better and better. Everything's going well. You sleep deeply. Everything is calm.

Third step: ascending

Give your subconscious a few days to get used to your new thoughts about sleep. You should notice a marked improvement in about a week.

What You Should Know

A few things should be said about the methods this book proposes to fight insomnia, because insomnia is above all a symptom. If you sleep badly, it's because something is wrong in your life. In other words, you sleep badly because you live badly.

It may happen that, after eliminating all the material and physical causes of your insomnia, you try the methods described above to get rid of the psychological causes – but without success.

If you persevere for a few weeks without success, it's either because you're not doing the exercises correctly (in which case it would be a good idea to go back and read the method through from the beginning, in case you've missed something or misunderstood an important point), or because your insomnia is the result of a more serious disorder, such as depression, which has to be treated. Treating the effect won't help if you don't look at the cause.

In any case, if your insomnia resists all attempts at a cure, talk to your doctor, who will very likely send you to a lab for tests.

But whatever the cause of your insomnia, avoid falling into the trap of relying on medication, and if you're already taking medication do everything possible to break the cycle of this dangerous dependence.

Finally, you should be aware that many people who say they're insomniacs aren't really. Though they may think they spend their nights wide awake staring up at the ceiling, they really do sleep for hours at a time. We don't all need the same amount of sleep, and the older we get, the less sleep we need.

If you feel perfectly well after sleeping for six hours, it means you don't need more than six hours' sleep. Take advantage of this natural gift to get a host of things done, or simply to meditate and relax. You should feel a little sorry for all those people who have to sleep two or three hours longer than you just to function as well.

CHAPTER 17

More Serious Illness and Disease

Up to now you've learnt to eliminate, through a variety of techniques, common health problems which are relatively benign, although some can cause acute pain and suffering. This chapter, on the other hand, is about serious illnesses, especially heart disease, cancer and AIDS.

The methods described here are based on the principle that we can play an active role in our own treatment even when the illness is serious and that our attitude is one of the determining factors of our recovery.

This approach supposes a broader relationship between doctor and patient. When faced with a long-term recovery programme, doctors often recommend leading a healthier life: stop smoking and drinking, eat moderately, be more active, and above all learn to live with a chronic disease.

But things change: at present, many psychologists believe this kind of general advice is not enough. The patient should contribute in a concrete way to his or her recovery, not only by regularly discussing various treatments with the doctor, but also by keeping a personal record of the disease, and above all by mobilizing all his or her psychological defences, by impressing the mind and body each day with the will to live.

That's what you'll learn to do in this chapter.

How to Regain a Healthy Heart

You've had a heart attack. You come home from hospital to convalesce, relieved to have survived. But the battle isn't over. You know you can have another heart attack at any time, and that it could be fatal.

The doctors have provided instructions on the kind of life you should lead to prevent another attack. That's fine, but you can do more.

WHY DO YOU HAVE A CARDIAC PROBLEM?

In about 85 per cent of cases, heart problems are related to lifestyle and stress. Statistics show that people who are moderately ambitious, who have some passionate interest, who are slim and physically active, do not suffer from heart problems unless the condition is hereditary.

Their blood pressure is normal or a little low, their cardiac muscles are well developed thanks to aerobic exercise, their cholesterol level is normal – and above all they are much less susceptible to stress and anxiety because of their moderate approach to life.

These people are also more likely to have a fulfilling and satisfying personal life, a factor which is very important in keeping the immune system in top shape.

YOUR CARDIAC RE-EDUCATION PROGRAMME

The programme in general looks like this:

- Learn to relax daily
- Follow an anti-stress programme
- Do daily visualization exercises to strengthen your heart and arterial system.

But be careful! This does not mean you can ignore your doctor's advice by resuming smoking and drinking, overeating and avoiding exercise. On the contrary, all your efforts should work together.

In most cases, people who smoked before their heart attack don't need to adhere to a specific programme to give up the bad habit afterwards. It seems that the fear caused by the attack is enough to discourage them from smoking altogether, or at least for a long time.

However, your doctor might also recommend losing some weight. Obesity is the cause of a host of problems. You can therefore add one of the weight loss techniques to your recovery programme (see Chapter 15). Your diet will be that much easier to follow, for two reasons:

- You'll lose weight faster, which is encouraging
- You will be able to change your tastes for food, and therefore avoid the energy loss which often accompanies following a strict diet.

A DAILY HABIT THAT CAN SAVE YOUR LIFE

Numerous relaxation exercises have been described in this book, and you may feel particularly attracted to one of them. However, for cardiac patients we strongly recommend the alpha relaxation method, and especially an exercise adapted from the 'heaviness' exercise (see Chapter 7) which we will call the 'weight and heat' technique. Why?

The sensation of heaviness means that the muscle or limb in question is completely relaxed. If you've had cardiac problems, we suggest adding the sensation of weight which results from the relaxation of the blood vessels.

Given that the sensation of heat does correspond to a modification in the physical state of your limbs, it becomes obvious that such a sensation in the left arm relaxes the blood vessels in and around the heart. Consquently your cardiac muscle dilates more easily, pumping more blood, which in turn reduces the risk of lesion and/or pain.

Here, then, is your complete relaxation exercise.

EXERCISE TO REGULATE BLOOD CIRCULATION

1. Get comfortable in a moderately heated room with the lights dimmed. Some people prefer sitting, with their back straight and their feet resting together on the floor. Others find it more comfortable to stretch out on the floor, or on a relatively hard mattress, with a small pillow to support the head and neck.
2. Loosen your clothing.
3. Make a conscious effort to do the 'heaviness' exercise (Chapter 7) from the beginning to the end of the second stage.
4. Now tell yourself that your right arm is getting warm. Repeat in your mind: 'My right arm is completely warm.' Continue until you actually feel a sensation of heat in your arm. To make it easier, you can first imagine yourself sitting in front of a wood fire. Visualize the fire, and yourself on a sofa near the fireplace. Or you can imagine that you're bathing each of your limbs in hot water.
5. Repeat the exercise with each of your four limbs, one after the other. You feel a pleasant warmth in your arms and legs.

6. Now go back to the point where you left off the 'heaviness' exercise (the beginning of the third stage), and mentally repeat the following message-shields:
   - 'My heart is beating regularly and normally.'
   - 'My heart is perfectly healthy.'
   - 'I'm feeling better and better.'
   - 'I'm perfectly calm.'
   - 'I'm relaxed.'
7. Finish the exercise as instructed in Chapter 7.

The combined 'weight and heat' exercise is especially recommended for people who have poor circulation in their extremities, and who always complain of having cold feet or hands. It is an excellent way to regularize the circulation.

A PRECIOUS ALLY: YOUR ANTI-STRESS PROGRAMME

To regain, and above all maintain, a healthy heart, you must combat stress. It is an essential condition of your recovery.

- In Chapter 11 you will find a very simple anti-stress programme which you would be well advised to start immediately.
- Two of the visualization exercises will help you rapidly to calm your irritated nerves and gradually acquire the serenity you lack. These are the ones on pp. 39–40, ('flexing') and p. 95 (the 'geyser').
- Do breathing exercises, which you should know very well by now, regularly.
- Walk a lot. Obviously when you come out of hospital you should avoid strenuous exercise, especially if you haven't done much before. But walking is the best thing you can do for yourself in your present condition. Walk as much as possible, at least an hour a day, in a quiet place (not in a city area full of car exhaust fumes) and breathe deeply. Make sure you visit your mental sanctuary at least once a day. Anything that helps you calm down is welcome.
- You should also try to get to the root of your stress problem by discovering and eliminating the causes. This is the ideal moment to take stock of your situation, of what you've accomplished up to now. And you will probably have to modify your priorities, being forced as you are to listen to your body as you've never done before.

HOW TO GET OPTIMUM RESULTS

Suffering a heart attack is an indication that you haven't been aware of your heart. You acted as if you didn't have one. You pushed it to its limit, without heeding its warning signals. It's time to change your attitude.

The exercises described in this section aim to:

- Make you conscious of the existence of your heart and the way it functions.
- Make your recovery programme as effective as possible.

Exercise to strengthen your heart

1. In an encyclopedia or medical dictionary, find an illustration of a healthy cardiac system.
2. Study it closely, and memorize it in detail.
3. Once a day, retreat to your mental sanctuary and do a few breathing exercises.
4. In your mind's eye, reconstruct the image of a cardio-vascular system in perfect health. This is your heart.
5. Look at it attentively. It is free of any lesions, it pumps out pure nourishing blood regularly and powerfully. Repeat to yourself that this intact cardio-vascular system is your own.

Exercise to clean your blood vessels

This exercise is especially effective if you suffer from arteriosclerosis.

1. Use your usual techniques to retreat to your mental sanctuary. Relax.
2. Imagine soft, supple tubes. A red liquid flows through these tubes – your blood. It is a pure, evenly flowing liquid. It flows like the water in a stream.
3. Look at your blood vessels. They're clean and smooth, with perfectly even walls.
4. Repeat to yourself that these healthy blood vessels are your own.

Fountain of health exercise

This is a great occasion to make use of your fountain of health. Proceed as usual, imagining that after diving into the fountain as a sick person you emerge healed, healthy, with a perfectly functioning heart.

SELF-HYPNOTIC CONDITIONING FOR CARDIAC RE-EDUCATION

You can apply the technique of self-hypnosis to get your heart back into shape and keep it that way. Proceed as usual, by taping your conditioning programme on a cassette.

First step: descending

Second step

1. Relax and breathe deeply, concentrating your attention on your heartbeat (with frequent pauses). Feel it beating regularly and calmly. Imagine the constant flow of blood passing through it. Your veins and arteries are carrying pure, nourishing, fluid blood. Your heart is a powerful pump. With each beat you feel your heart getting stronger, as it becomes more and more healthy and powerful.
2. Your cardiovascular system is purified. Your arteries are free of obstructions. Your blood flows freely through them. Your heart is healthy. Your arteries are healthy. You feel good and strong. Everything is fine.
3. You feel each heartbeat. Your heart is strong. It does its work perfectly. You can depend on it. It is powerful, it's healthy, it's full of energy. It beats regularly and calmly. It is strong.
4. Repeat the second step.

Third step: ascending

1. Don't tone down your efforts. You and you alone are responsible for the state of your heart. Love your heart, care for it, and give it all the attention you've been withholding for the last few years. It will respond to your care, you can be certain.

A Different Approach to Cancer

At present, it is estimated that between 30 and 40 per cent of cancers are curable. But the technology used to fight the illness is sometimes frightening, and the side-effects of certain treatments are so unpleasant that patients fear the treatment as much as the disease itself, and rightly so.

WHY DO PEOPLE GET CANCER?

Cancer begins with the appearance of a cell which contains faulty genetic information, either because it has been influenced by toxic substances, or because it has been damaged by exterior factors, or for some unknown reason. If this cell reproduces itself into other faulty cells, a tumour is formed. Under ordinary circumstances our immune system recognizes these cells and destroys them immediately, or makes their propagation impossible. But when our natural defences are weakened, for one reason or another, the disease spreads.

Our immune system is extraordinarily powerful. Its commando units are composed of white blood cells, known as leucocytes, which are always on the alert. Without our knowing, they are waging a constant battle to protect our bodies against all kinds of attacks. So if you have cancer, the reason is not only that abnormal cells are forming in your body, but also that your immune system is not functioning as it should.

Researchers have discovered that a certain reaction to various kinds of stress favours, among other factors, the appearance a few months later of cancerous cells. To summarize a complex process, a negative and depressive reaction to stress results in:

1. hormonal imbalances which tend to encourage the production of abnormal cells
2. a weakening of our natural defences.

HOW TO ACCELERATE RECOVERY

To accelerate the healing process, you must take an active part in your recovery.

- Start by making a personal record of your disease and of the treatments that are prescribed. If your doctor doesn't want to explain things to you, find another one. When someone is stricken with a potentially fatal disease, he or she has the right to know how the treatment works.
- Eliminate stress-causing factors from your life. Take energetic measures to establish your priorities, and get all possible advantages on your side. Follow the anti-stress programme described in Chapter 11.
- Don't let yourself go. Make plans for the future, set goals for yourself. Treat your recovery as a *fait accompli*.

- Get as much out of your amorous and amicable relationships as possible, with both family and friends. In other words, set up a psychological and emotional support network for yourself.
- Get rid of feelings of hate, jealousy, disdain — any destructive emotions.
- Finally, do every day the exercises you have learnt. They are based mainly on:
  - Relaxation
  - Visualization
  - Self-hypnotic conditioning.

Progressive relaxation exercise

This exercise is described in detail in Chapter 10 (p. 66). We recommend beginning all your exercise sessions with this technique, because it gets you into the best possible state for benefiting from the exercises that follow.

Anti-cancer visualization exercise

1. Get comfortable in your mental retreat.
2. Imagine the struggle taking place between your leucocytes and the abnormal cells. You can use any images you like, or those which are easiest for you to produce.
3. Your forces are ferocious and tireless. There's no doubt they will win the battle. You can see them clearly.
4. Next, imagine the cancerous cells. Don't visualize them as being ferocious and aggressive, but rather as weak, malformed wretches with hardly any power. You see them scattered and destroyed by your army. Imagine that they are totally eliminated from the field of battle and secreted out of your body through your natural orifices.
5. Continue the fight until all the cancerous cells have been entirely eliminated from the battlefield.
6. Now imagine yourself in perfect health, happy, loving and completely cured.

Exercise to reinforce your medical treatment

In this exercise you will visualize the effects of the medical treatment you are receiving on your body, and thus reinforce its effects.

1. Retreat to your mental sanctuary in the usual way.
2. Visualize your treatment in a way that's easily comprehensible. For example, if you're being treated with chemotherapy, imagine the substances circulating in your blood and poisoning the cancerous cells, which are stupid and weak, while your healthy cells do not allow themselves to fall into the trap. If you're getting radiation treatment, imagine the rays hitting the cells in its path. Your healthy cells are invulnerable, while the malignant cells disintegrate under the powerful ray . . . and so on.
3. If you don't know exactly how the treatment you're getting works, ask your doctor to explain it to you. You must be able to visualize it clearly and easily.

Note: as you've no doubt understood, you can reinforce the effects of any kind of treatment. If you're suffering from another type of serious or chronic illness, don't hesitate to ask your doctor to explain the principle of the treatment, and join the offensive against your illness by practising your exercises every day.

Exercise to reduce or eliminate a tumour

1. Retreat to your mental sanctuary.
2. Now imagine that your cancer is a large block of ice.
3. Suddenly, the sun appears. Feel its heat, see its rays shining like gold.
4. It shines on the block of ice. Little by little, the block starts to melt, slowly but steadily. It melts. Your cancer is melting, disappearing little by little.
5. Continue until there isn't one drop of water left where the block of ice was before.

Use self-hypnosis to develop your healing powers

You can also use a hypnotic conditioning exercise designed to command your subconscious to create an obstacle to what is happening in your body. It is, of course, a gradual process, because tumours don't disappear overnight. But if you persevere, you will be well rewarded.

The self-hypnotic conditioning which you will use, a model of which is described below, must result in your:

- relaxing
- visualizing positive images of the struggle of your body against the disease (you may use the same images as those you've just learnt for the immune system 'battle')
- visualize positive images which increase your sense of wellbeing, and which take your recovery for granted
- ordering your subconscious to keep you in good health, no matter what.

Here's a model of a conditioning exercise which you can adapt or use as it is.

First step: descending

Second step

1. Concentrate your attention on the cancerous zone. Imagine your natural defences fighting the cancer cells. Describe the fight, using your own images.
2. Now imagine that the cancer is defeated. Your cancerous cells retreat in total disarray, they are defeated, they vanish over the horizon, fleeing to distant regions from which they can never return.
3. Now imagine your tissues freed of their burden, healthy again, clean and normal. Your treatment has worked and you're cured. You're in great health. You feel stronger and stronger, better and better. You smile. You see yourself smiling, happy, in perfect health, active and full of energy. You are cured.
4. Repeat stages 2 and 3.

Third step: ascending

The Problem of AIDS

AIDS is the disease which is most closely related to the breakdown of the immune system and the inability of our self-healing powers to correct the situation. However, it is possible to trigger your natural defences even if you are diagnosed as having AIDS.

One person who got AIDS and cured herself is Niro Markoff Asistent, whose extraordinary story of self-healing – from HIV positive to HIV negative – is documented in her book *Why I Survive AIDS*. It shows that techniques such as self-hypnosis and meditation are powerful enough to cure a disease as devastating as AIDS.

Once she was diagnosed as HIV positive, Niro significantly altered her lifestyle. She began to meditate daily. She changed to a healthy diet and started to exercise regularly. She also used another technique which apparently she discovered intuitively. This was visualization.

Visualization for AIDS

Niro developed the ability to see inside her body. She saw her liver, her stomach, and her other internal organs. But their colour was a putrid shade of yellowish green.

How could she remove this colour? Every day, she visualized the Niagara Falls flushing away all that disgusting green from inside her body.

You can adapt the cancer self-hypnosis induction given on pp. 166–7 to include this visualization.

Niro had another interesting daily routine.

The 3 daily goals

No matter how bad she felt, Niro always committed herself to accomplish these things every day. She settled for three simple goals that she knew she could achieve. Try this technique. Your 'goal' might be writing a letter, repairing something, sewing on a missing button, etc. If you achieve each of these goals it means that you have kept your word to yourself and this will allow you to feel that your life is in order. If you believe in yourself, you increasingly believe that it is possible for you to be healed.

Another Curse of the Century: Depression

You will find a good definition of depression, as seen by a depressive person, in the work of the French author Chateaubriand who wrote: 'With a heavy heart we inhabit an empty world, and without ever enjoying anything, we ourselves are abused and exhausted by it all.' Today more than ever, depression has become a destructive force in all strata of society.

Let's say you're being treated for depression by a psychotherapist, and that, most important, you firmly intend to get rid of the problem. Actually, this is not always the case. The biggest problem therapists have in treating depression is that the patient doesn't always want to get better. Even if a person agrees to be treated and to take concrete measures, he or she often retains a deep-seated desire to prolong the illness.

If you read this, it should be because you *want* to get better. You want to regain your appetite for life and happiness.

HOW TO GET RID OF DEPRESSION

The programme presented here can be followed as a complement to your psychotherapy treatments and will help you reinforce its effects. To climb back up the hill and rediscover your love for life, you must eliminate any defeatist attitudes you have developed. Therefore learn to get rid of negative, pessimistic thoughts. For a few weeks do the exercise on pp. 80–1.

Visit your sanctuary every day

It is of paramount importance when dealing with depression that you possess a sanctuary, a decompression chamber, a place where you can exclude everything that you find displeasing. Each day, take a moment to relax and do breathing exercises. Practise rhythmic breathing and allow a peaceful feeling of wellbeing to spread through you.

Relax daily

Relaxation, as you know, helps you decompress completely and liberates your mind. It will allow you to reach a level of serenity that will persist for some hours after you do the exercises. You can use any of the methods described in this book. The main thing is that they work for you, and help you purify yourself of all the mental toxins that disturb your equilibrium.

Fighting dark thoughts

Use the blackboard–white board method to get rid of your defeatist thoughts. For example, on the blackboard you can write thoughts like:

- 'Nothing interests me. . .'
- 'The weather's always bad. . .'
- 'I'm not good at what I do. . .'
- 'I'm a drag. . .'
- 'I feel so lethargic. . .'
- 'I can't depend on anyone. . .'

Use the white board to write your positive thoughts, which you want to impress on your subconscious:

- 'I like (insert any activity you enjoy, but which you haven't had the courage to do). . .'
- 'Even if the weather's bad now, it won't last, and anyway it isn't important. . .'
- 'I do my work as well as possible, and I'm no more incompetent than anyone else. . .'

Persevere with this method. You can use the three-month cycle if you think an extended programme will be beneficial. At the end of this period, you should feel a real improvement in your general attitude.

If you feel tired

When people are depressed, they carry an enormous burden of fatigue – usually invented – on their shoulders. They don't do anything because they think they feel tired, and they feel tired because they don't do anything. You need to break this vicious circle.

In Chapter 11 you will find on pp. 83–4 a short anti-fatigue programme, consisting of two especially pleasant and invigorating visualization exercises: overcoming fatigue and recharging your batteries. On days when you feel especially lazy or down, add them to your programme.

But, most important, don't be inactive. It is biologically impossible to be depressed when engaged in some kind of physical endurance exercise. Take charge of yourself and get going on some activity that you like. In the past people tended to confuse sports with competition. Fortunately things have changed. We can enjoy sports and exercise without having the slightest desire to compete against others. The simple act of walking briskly for an hour a day, or of avoiding escalators and lifts and climbing the stairs instead, is a step in the right direction.

Enjoy yourself

You must have noticed the charge you can get out of buying something new, or getting a new hairstyle. Make these kinds of things part of your therapy.

Go shopping for clothes that you like and that will enhance your appearance. You don't have to spend a fortune. Just buy yourself a little something now and then – something frivolous that isn't necessarily expensive.

As far as stuffing yourself with food – take this piece of advice. When people are depressed they often tend to eat too much, and especially to indulge between meals. If you are suddenly overcome with the desire to eat the first piece of sticky gâteau you can get your hands on, go and buy a scarf or a tie or a T-shirt instead of an éclair. You'll get the same kick minus the calories.

Whether you're male or female, a massage session will be very pleasant and do you a lot of good. Offer yourself this little luxury from time to time. It doesn't cost as much as you think. Both your body and your mind will benefit.

Self-hypnosis

You can also make good use of hypnotic conditioning to treat depression. Tape a session and, as usual, listen to it when you go to bed each night. In a few weeks you'll wake up singing instead of frowning. Frame the middle section between the descent and ascent, as usual.

First step: descending

Second step

- You are relaxed, very relaxed and calm. Everything around you is calm. You feel good. You are confident. Your life is full of hope and promise. You're proud of what you've accomplished up to now. You will continue being proud. Your life is pleasant, calm, full of hope.
- You are relaxed and calm. You feel happy. Everything is going well. You feel good about yourself. You await the future with confidence. Everything is fine, everything is calm.
- You feel strong, full of energy, healthy. Everything in your life is going well. You like what you do. Your life is happy and serene.

You know what it is to be peaceful. You feel good about yourself. You have confidence in the future.

Third step: ascending

It's possible that, with the help of your therapist, you've succeeded in bringing to the surface precise factors which are causing your depression. If so, and with the therapist's approval, it might be wise to insert a few messages into your conditioning which will neutralize their negative effects.

Climbing Back up the Hill – Your Personal Programme

It is possible to set up a programme to deal with almost any kind of serious or chronic illness, which can be adapted from the guidelines given below to suit the patient's individual temperament and tastes.

ELIMINATE STRESS

The role that stress plays in causing a host of disorders cannot be overstated. Therefore, your personal programme should begin by easing the stress that is eating away at your health.

- Learn to relax, and use one (or a number) of the relaxation methods described in this book on a daily basis.
- Try to learn to meditate by applying one of the methods in this book.
- Follow the anti-stress programme (Chapter 11).
- Do the exercises designed to calm your nerves (Chapter 12).
- Eliminate causes of stress from your day-to-day life, even if it means making major changes like moving, changing jobs, altering your schedule etc.
- Review your priorities and decide, once and for all, what you want out of life.

TAKE YOUR RECOVERY FOR GRANTED

This is where psychocybernetics and/or self-hypnosis comes in. After reading about the exercises designed to treat people with cardiac problems or cancer, you should have a pretty good idea of the path you should follow. Whatever your problem is, adapt the exercise to suit it by imagining the illness as a concrete, identifiable entity which can be defeated by your natural defences.

Here's another exercise which you can do *after* the fighting exercise, or in isolation, whenever you have a few quiet moments.

Purification exercise

1. In your mental sanctuary, imagine that a beam of golden light is shining down on you.
2. The beam grows larger and envelops your entire body from top to bottom. You can see it perfectly clearly.
3. The light penetrates your body through your pores. It shines everywhere, on all your organs, on your muscles, your blood, your nerves, on all your cells. Look at it closely.
4. The light cleans your whole organism. It purifies all your cells and washes your blood clean. You feel its gentle heat penetrating the tiniest recesses of your body. It enters your lungs, cleaning and purifying them. Then it moves to your stomach, and finally into your intestines, cleaning away all the impurities in its path. The cleansing light repeats its journey through your body a number of times.
5. The golden light makes you strong, healthy and happy. When its work is done, it departs from your body slowly and then dissolves. It leaves you with a peaceful, calm feeling. You are cured.

DON'T LET THINGS GET YOU DOWN

This is the greatest danger one has to face when seriously ill. And in the final analysis, it is a very understandable reaction to disease. But if you want to get better, you must not allow this kind of attitude to take root in your system. If your attitude is defeatist from the start, how do you think your subconscious will react when exposed to such negative images?

- Keep making plans for the future. Live for the present, of course, but plan to do pleasant things. Anticipate the future with a sense of enthusiasm.
- Be optimistic. Do the exercise described on pp. 80–1 regularly.
- Love and be loved. Set up a support network of people around you. Don't shut yourself up in a shell. Be open to others and accept the love and friendship they offer.

- If there are certain leisure activities which you've always wanted to do but never had time for, the moment has come to make room for them. But don't blow up their importance out of proportion, so that they limit you as much as you were limited by other matters before. Just get rid of all the things that are not essential in your life, and replace them with activities that you enjoy.

COME TO TERMS WITH YOUR BODY

When we suddenly discover we have a serious or chronic illness, it is natural to feel a certain amount of animosity towards our body which, in a sense, seems to have betrayed us, even if we accept that the origin of most illnesses lies in the brain.

Here are a few ideas about measures you can take to come to terms with your body.

- Take care of your appearance. Buy clothes that you like. Dress to please yourself.
- Pamper your body. In a culture as hedonistic as our own, opportunities are certainly not lacking (massages, beauty treatments etc.).
- Don't suppress your sexuality under the pretext of being sick. Talk about it openly to your doctor, or consult a sex therapist, either alone or with your partner. Some illnesses do require a certain adaptation process, and you must know exactly what to expect.

AN ALTERNATIVE LIFESTYLE

It's obvious that, although you may do your visualization exercises regularly and practise meditation every day for ten years, if you persist in eating a family-sized tub of ice cream a day you'll never get rid of your gastric ulcers! Similarly, if you drink fifteen cups of coffee a day no programme of self-hypnosis can keep you out of hospital after suffering an attack of hypertension. You have to do your part. Your recovery is based on a combination of interdependent factors.

- Make yourself eat a balanced diet. Your doctor will have advised you about what and what not to eat.
- Needless to say, it's now or never for giving up smoking.
- Exercise regularly. Even if you're limited to an hour of walking per day by your illness or the treatment you're getting, do it. Move! Do yoga or gymnastics to keep your limbs and joints supple. If you're not supposed to do anything strenuous, ask

your doctor to provide a programme suited to your condition, so you avoid making any mistakes.

- Stick to a regular schedule. Try to go to bed and wake up at the same time every day, so as not to upset your internal clock. If you have to work nights or irregular shifts, try to minimize the disturbance. It is known that the hours we spend sleeping before midnight are most important to the body's recovery. So it's better to get up very early than to go to bed very late.
- Develop your sense of humour. Laughter is excellent therapy. Read funny books, go to comic movies, spend time with amusing people. A good burst of laughter every day will only reinforce the beneficial effects of your personal programme.

According to my calculations, my heart has beat 876,946,280 times more than the doctors at my insurance company predicted it would. I met someone on a New York streetcorner, one of the specialists who had diagnosed the sad case of my progressive paralysis. His surprise at seeing me was obvious. He was very curious to have me explain my recovery. I told him it all started the day I decided certain so-called experts just didn't know enough to condemn a human being to death.

Professor Norman Cousins, *The Will to Recover*

(Norman Cousins used laughter and positive emotions to full advantage in curing himself. He watched comic films for weeks, read humorous books, and complemented this form of mental treatment with massive doses of Vitamin C. His case brought him 3000 congratulatory letters from doctors around the world, and a position on the Faculty of Medicine at the University of California in Los Angeles.)

How to Master Your Emotions and Be Positive

Are you short-tempered? Do you get on your high horse whenever someone suggests an idea contrary to your way of thinking, or dares to criticize you? Do you lack self-confidence? In this chapter you'll learn how to apply to these kinds of problems the methods described in the first part of the book. Although this isn't a treatment as such, you will be aware that your state of mind, your sense of personal fulfilment or frustration, and your psychological and emotional traumas, are all important factors which contribute to health or illness. Therefore the suggestions presented here can be considered as a kind of preventive therapy. By caring for your emotions and feelings, you reinforce your natural immune system.

How to Master Your Temperament

It's not a good idea to suppress anger – because turned inward, it can only become more dangerous. Anger is there to protect you. Your personal territory, your possessions. Without it you would be defenceless. A pushover.

THE DANGERS OF SUPPRESSED ANGER

When a volcano erupts, people in the region much prefer the crater not to be blocked up, and the lava to be allowed to flow freely. If not, the gases which would accumulate underground would eventually explode, and that would be catastrophic.

Suppressed anger is comparable to a blocked volcano. If you have an angry temperament, it's useless to try and suppress a crisis. If you do, the time will come when it will explode anyway, only a thousand times worse, destroying everything in its path.

And it will destroy you too. If you don't allow yourself to express your anger towards others, it will turn back on yourself. We've been conditioned since childhood with messages like, 'It's not good to get angry. . . . Boys and girls who are well brought up don't get angry. . . . Only bad children get angry . . . etc.' So if we feel angry we tend to punish ourselves with all sorts of self-destructive behaviour like smoking, drinking, biting our nails, overeating, anorexia, drugs, enuresis. . . . The list of forms of self-punishment goes on and on.

Therefore you're going to learn not how to suppress your anger, but how to channel it.

HOW TO CHANNEL YOUR ANGER

The best method consists of representing your anger as a force of nature, and letting it exhaust itself. You can then regain and maintain your peace of mind.

First stage: the soothing image

Use a tangible visual image

Start by looking through books and magazines for large-format images of the forces of nature at work. Choose a natural phenomenon that you find particularly appealing. It could be a hurricane, a waterfall thundering over a cliff, a tornado, a blizzard, a geyser, an avalanche or a tidal wave. You may prefer a painting or engraving to a real photograph, depending on your taste.

Then continue as follows:

1. As soon as you feel your anger rising, whether it's the kind that explodes or just a smouldering hate, turn to your image.
2. Get comfortable on a chair or sofa and look at the image.
3. Imagine it moving, as if you were really watching the spectacle of this amazingly powerful force of nature first-hand. See the towering waves, the wind twisting and uprooting trees, the water crashing down from the top of a cliff.

4. After a moment, lift your eyes and do a few breathing exercises. You should feel your anger abating.
5. Do this exercise a few times a day if you feel you have a lot of aggression to channel.

Use the power of your mind

This exercise is based on the same principle as the previous one, except that you'll be able to do it anywhere, any time, without relying on a photograph or other image. You will create the image in your own mind.

1. Get comfortable, preferably in your mental sanctuary.
2. Do a few breathing exercises.
3. Now imagine a force of nature at work. Choose one which relates to your personality and taste. The important thing is to see it very clearly.
4. After a few moments, do some more breathing exercises and feel yourself relaxing.
5. Repeat the exercise as often as necessary.

Second stage: once you've regained your calm

After getting into the habit of regularly doing one of the above exercises (or both) for a few weeks, you will feel that your life is becoming easier. You sleep better, and you probably digest your food better. Now you must consolidate your success.

First of all learn to relax

Spending a few minutes each day relaxing, whatever the method you adopt, frees your mind of numerous toxins. You purify it, and it becomes less susceptible to anger and much more tolerant.

Choose a meditation technique

By elevating you to a higher spiritual plane, meditation transforms you into what was, in other times, called a 'sage'. Through meditation you will automatically learn to anticipate the reactions of others. Therefore, if your anger is mainly caused by your reaction to others' behaviour, you will no longer have any reason to get mad.

You will also sort out what is and is not important in your life. You won't get upset about trivialities any more. You will accept others more easily, while learning also to accept yourself.

Finally, doing meditation will allow you to purify yourself of all the suppressed anger you've accumulated over the years, which is the most important part.

But you have to do your share and devote at least twenty minutes a day to some kind of meditation exercise, for a period of several weeks. You can't get rid of the poisons which have been circulating inside you for years in a couple of days.

Regain Your Memory

It is no secret that, as we we get older, our memories start to resemble a piece of Swiss cheese full of holes. Even people who could boast of having a phenomenal memory when they were young end up by falling into the bitter trap of experiencing 'memory blanks'.

However, the information that your conscious mind has seemingly forgotten can still be found, stored away in the subconscious. The subconscious records everything and forgets nothing. The problem consists of knowing how to access this information, which is no longer spontaneously available.

If you've ever used a computer, you probably know about those little programs designed to recover files which have been erased from the disc by mistake. If you think of your subconscious as that disc then all you have to do is design a program to recover those lost files.

PROCEDURE FOR IMPROVING YOUR MEMORY

The best method consists of using self-hypnotic conditioning, which allows you to communicate your instructions directly to the subconscious. You can create your own programme by using the example below as a model. It should contain mainly affirmative messages. Proceed as usual by taping the three steps without interruption.

PROGRAMME FOR REGAINING MEMORY

First step: descending

Second step

1. You are relaxed, very relaxed. All is well and calm. Your memory is improving daily. You have a good memory, a dependable memory.

You can count on your memory because it's getting more and more dependable.

2. Imagine your memory in the form of a fruit, any fruit. It is healthy, perfectly smooth, free of imperfections. It's perfect. This is your memory.

3. Your memory is dependable. You can count on it. It becomes more and more dependable every day. You are happy with the progress your memory is making.

4. Repeat from the beginning.

Third step: ascending

Persevere, and you will see your memory improve tremendously.

Self-confidence

Lack of self-confidence is the cause of numerous problems. It can lead to stagefright and insomnia, destroy our personal relationships, upset our digestion, reduce our professional productivity – in short it can ruin our lives.

However, unless you're superhuman you have your weak points just like everyone else. We rarely meet someone who is totally self-assured in all ways, and if we do we usually discover that the person is just putting up a good front.

Confidence is essential for attaining and maintaining happiness and mental equilibrium. And a lack of self-confidence can be rectified.

HOW TO ACQUIRE MORE CONFIDENCE

Start by determining which aspects of your life reveal the greatest lack of self-confidence. The problem might be general for some, but for most of us it is related to a specific area of behaviour, whether at work, in personal relationships, at school or in relations with the opposite sex.

When you know in exactly which area to direct your reprogramming, devote a few minutes each day to the exercises.

Blackboard–white board exercise

Once again, this simple technique can be of enormous help. Proceed in the usual way, which you should be fully familiar with by now. Write your negative thoughts on the blackboard, as concisely as possible. Don't be afraid to tell the truth – no one else will see what you write. Don't hesitate to open doors which you've fearfully kept closed until now. Explore your mind fully, right to the limit.

For example, if your lack of self-confidence manifests itself mostly in your relationships with the opposite sex, you can write thoughts on the blackboard like: 'I was rejected once, and I'm afraid of being rejected again. . .'; 'I'm not physically attractive. . .'; 'I'm afraid of being impotent. . .' etc. It is essential that you be frank with yourself, and that you hide none of your most secret thoughts.

After reading and rereading these negative thoughts, accompanied by feelings of disapproval and disgust for them, destroy the blackboard. Now write your positive thoughts on the white board.

To continue our example, you may write things like: 'Being rejected once means nothing. . .'; 'I have nothing to be ashamed of as far as my physical appearance goes. . .'; 'There's no reason why I should be impotent. . .' etc.

Do the exercise over a three-month cycle to reinforce your growing confidence.

Dynamism exercise

Another very effective exercise consists of invoking your subconscious after having recharged your psychic energy.

1. Retreat to your mental sanctuary.
2. Now imagine a sphere of golden light above your head. It descends and surrounds you like an aura. It protects you and at the same time charges you with energy.
3. When you are entirely surrounded by the light, communicate with your subconscious in short, concise sentences, such as:
   - 'I have confidence in myself.'
   - 'My confidence is growing day by day.'
   - 'I'm at my best.'
   - 'This is who I *am*!'
   - 'I like myself just the way I am.'
   - 'I'm proud of myself.'
4. Now provide precise instructions concerning those aspects of your personality which you've decided are your weak points, for example:
   - 'I am competent.'
   - 'I'm an excellent worker.'

- 'I have complete confidence in my competence.'
- 'I am a success. . .' etc.

5. Now imagine that the golden light fades little by little. You are in your sanctuary, and you breathe the pure air.

This very positive exercise is both relaxing and dynamic. It recharges you and creates a feeling of profound wellbeing.

Responding better to Criticism

Is this a sensitive point with you? Are you one of those people who are sensitive to the least criticism?

When someone passes judgement on you and expresses an opinion about you, you know right away whether that opinion is justified or not, and it's completely normal to be offended by an unjust opinion. Nevertheless some criticism, even when exaggerated, can be instructive by opening new doors and horizons which we never thought about before. So there's something positive to be found in most criticism.

Some people can take criticism without getting upset. Unfortunately they are getting harder and harder to find, disdained as they are by our society, which rewards aggressiveness and not passivity.

If you have trouble accepting criticism, it's probably because you lack self-confidence. You're not sure of what you're doing. Whenever someone points out one of your mistakes, or suggests that you do things differently, you react by getting angry or confused.

Therefore, begin with the programme described in the preceding section on self-confidence. You have to learn to stop feeling persecuted every time someone makes a slightly critical remark about you. This will probably be the most difficult part of your programme. Whenever someone says something about you, you will make a conscious effort to react in the same, disciplined way, having practised a programme consisting first of some visualization exercises to teach you how to deal with a hypothetical situation. You will then adapt your reactions to a real situation, so that you handle it calmly.

HOW TO STAY CALM

1. Get comfortable and relax.
2. Visualize a situation where you are criticized or insulted.

3. Now imagine that the criticisms levelled at you take the form of a particular kind of missile – one that can't hurt you. You can visualize them as blank bullets, rubber-tipped arrows, paper planes . . . whatever you like. You see them clearly as they fall around you, without harming you in the least.
4. When you get used to visualizing such imaginary situations, apply the process to a real situation. If you find yourself the target of criticism, compare what is being said to the harmless projectiles of your imagination. In a short time you will feel that you've mastered the situation.

Evidently, to succeed in this you have to stay calm. If you feel yourself becoming exasperated and spiteful despite your efforts to remain calm, resort to the 'geyser and flexing' exercises (pp. 39–40, 95) which will allow you to let off some steam in a harmless way.

TURN CRITICISM TO YOUR ADVANTAGE

You can also arrange to corner the person criticizing you so that he or she can't shy away after launching their barbed comments. Let's take an example. Say your boss is criticizing your work.

First step

Neutralize your critic: 'I really wanted to know your opinion. I respect your suggestions because you have so much more experience in the field than I do.' etc.

Second step

Force your critic to reveal his true motives. Don't let him escape after he's spat a few drops of venom at you. If the criticism is not constructive or valid, you'll know immediately. In that case be magnanimous, but politely affirm your position.

Third step

If the suggestions are made in good faith, study them and discusss them with your critic. Don't just turn on your heel and swallow the offence against you.

By adopting this simple attitude, which requires an effort of will on your part, you will soon become aware that the feelings of outrage you experienced in the past when faced with criticism have abated. Persevere, and they'll disappear completely.

How to Succeed at School, at Work and in Sport

Self-confidence naturally plays a large role in achieving success professionally, academically or in sport. It is an antidote for fear, stagefright, inferiority complexes and so on. So the first thing to do is to follow the short programme on self-confidence in this chapter. Then adapt certain very precise visualization exercises to your particular situation.

ACHIEVEMENT EXERCISE

1. As usual, retreat to your mental sanctuary.
2. Now visualize yourself doing your work, or studying, or writing an essay, or running the hundred yards – whatever you want to work on.
3. When these images are perfectly clear, visualize yourself in the act of succeeding at whatever you're doing. For example, your boss or teacher is congratulating you, or you win your race. If you don't practise any competitive sports, you can picture yourself doing some sport that you enjoy with great skill and superb technique . . . and so on.
4. Let a moment pass during which you experience all the exhilaration of your success, and then return to your sanctuary.

HOW TO ATTAIN YOUR OBJECTIVE

1. Get comfortable, and relax using your preferred method.
2. Imagine the event in your professional, academic or sports life that you wish to create. This event is already a *fait accompli* in your mind's eye.
3. Now imagine a golden bubble in which you place your image of success.
4. Imagine that this bubble, which contains your wish, flies away. It is

free, it floats up into the air. It will attract all the energy it needs to make your wish a reality.
5. When the bubble has disappeared over the horizon, open your eyes.

HOW TO IMPROVE YOURSELF

Even if you are a success at work, at school or in sports, you certainly still have the desire to do even better. Improving yourself is a praiseworthy and altogether attainable objective. Here's an exercise that will support your efforts daily.

Success exercise

1. Take the time you need to relax, using the technique you like best. Your mind should be completely open and free of any outside problems.
2. Next, visualize yourself in the act of doing the activity in question. Your image should be perfectly clear.
3. Now imagine the progress you make. Your mastery grows and you do the work easily.
4. Visualize yourself improving every day. You see the progress you make from one day to the next. For example, if you want to improve your skiing, imagine that you're surging downhill, your movements supple and harmonious, almost effortless. If you're a sales rep, see yourself as entirely convincing, dynamic, irresistible, in the act of closing a big deal.

You can rest assured that when something is important to us, it's very easy to create images of improvement and success.

Make Your Personal Life a Success

It's all in the mind – to attain satisfaction in your personal life, you must start off a winner. You will succeed by considering your success as something already accomplished. The three keys to emotional success are:

- Optimism
- Confidence in yourself and in others
- Love of life.

OPTIMISM

It's normal to experience crises at certain periods in our lives, but we must not allow our fundamental attitude to be shaken. The success of your personal life depends on your attitude towards this all too short life.

Make optimism your guiding principle. If you think you're lacking optimism, don't just say, 'I'm a born pessimist, I can't do anything about it. . .'. Something can be done. Turn to Chapter 11 and learn how gradually to remedy your pessimistic attitude.

CONFIDENCE IN YOURSELF AND IN OTHERS

If you don't have confidence in your partner, it's really because you lack confidence in yourself, in your capacity to keep being loved. And if you lack self-confidence, you will inevitably lose confidence in your partner. Therefore the two factors – confidence in yourself and in others – are closely linked.

Start by following the instructions on self-confidence earlier in this chapter. Then, if you feel that still isn't enough to consolidate your relationship, turn to the advice in Chapter 13, in the section on overcoming jealousy.

LOVE OF LIFE

This heading may at first seem surprising in a section dealing with your personal life, but you will soon understand that it makes perfect sense to consider love of life one of the keys to emotional success.

Happiness doesn't fall from the sky. It's a state of mind, a collection of positive thoughts which occur either spontaneously, or because you've made an effort to program yourself in a positive direction. Love of life is the knot which unites all these positive thoughts and feelings, whose combined energy forms what we call happiness.

How many people do you know who are grateful just to be alive, to love and be loved, to experience the beauty of nature, of the sky and the stars, the seasons? No doubt very few.

Be one of those people. It is proof of a great inner strength. By loving and being grateful for life, you will never become disillusioned or arrogant. You will remain perpetually enchanted by the love you received and the love you give.

Each time you have a moment, close your eyes, take a deep breath and say to yourself: 'Thank you.'

CHAPTER · 19

How to Contribute to Your Children's Development

Whether you're a parent or teacher, you will certainly find some use in the application of psychocybernetic techniques to problems relating to children. The basic principles are the same as those encountered in the methods you've just learnt, but certain adaptations are necessary.

Psychocybernetics can really help solve a number of problems which parents find exasperating: bedwetting, fear of the dark or of being alone, poor academic performance, inattentiveness in class, fear of domestic animals, habits like biting nails or thumb sucking, bulimia, sugar addiction and a host of others.

Learn to Influence Your Child

HIS (OR HER) PERSONAL SANCTUARY

The first step consists of helping the child consciously discover his own mental sanctuary. Choose a time of day when the child is calm but receptive, and get comfortable with him in a quiet room. Make him lie down next to you and close his eyes.

When he's relaxed, get him to imagine his retreat, according to his personal tastes. It could be a magnificent garden, or a mysterious cave, a cabin in the woods or on a mountaintop. Help him to describe the sanctuary in detail, and to feel all the physical sensations associated with the place, sensations of touch, taste, smell and sound, as well as sight.

Don't be surprised if the child shows an extraordinary ability to visualize and experience detailed images. Children love what they consider new games, and are much more spontaneous than adults because they've had less time to be limited by rigid codes of conduct and thinking. In their world, the fantastic and the imaginary are often more accessible than reality.

MAKE SUGGESTIONS WHILE THE CHILD IS ASLEEP

When your child is used to retreating to his mental sanctuary in your company, you can start making suggestions while he is asleep.

Wait a few minutes after he's fallen asleep. He will then be in the alpha state. This is the moment when he is most open to suggestion, because he will hear everything you say.

Start talking as soon as you enter the room. Gently approach the bed. Speak very softly, so that your voice is barely audible. Take him to his sanctuary, which you are perfectly familiar with. Describe it, omitting no details.

Then start to formulate your suggestions according to the principles you've learnt in this book:

- No negations, only positive affirmations;
- No commands, just affirmations;
- Short, simple, clear sentences.

For example, if your child cries every time he goes to bed because he's afraid of the dark, you could suggest something like:

- You like going to sleep at night.
- The dark is your friend, it helps you rest.
- You know you're going to sleep very well tonight.
- It gets dark so you can go to sleep . . . etc.

PATIENCE

Be patient. You may need a few sessions to change your child's behaviour, especially if you've already tried other, more conventional ways to remedy the problem (reprimands, threats, spankings, punishment and reward and so on), which are usually traumatic and only serve to worsen the condition. But you should see an improvement within a few weeks.

Remember: if you have a number of problems to resolve, wait for one to be eliminated before starting on another. Just as with adults, children's subconscious minds cannot deal with more than one problem at a time.

THE BLACKBOARD METHOD: IT WORKS FOR KIDS TOO

For slighter older children and adolescents, the blackboard–white board technique works extremely well.

Let's say, for example, that you're worried about your child's schoolwork. He or she may be a bit careless, or lazy, or not interested enough in school. Whatever the reason, the method of the two boards will give him a taste for doing good work. Here's how to proceed:

1. Retreat with your child to his mental sanctuary.
2. Show him the two boards, one black, the other white.
3. Explain how to use the white chalk to write his negative thoughts about school on the blackboard. Make it clear that he'll be the only person to see them, and that no one else can enter his sanctuary. It's important that the child should not be afraid to explore his mind honestly. He could write things like, 'I can't concentrate in class. . .' or 'The subject doesn't interest me. . .' or 'I can't do my homework at night. . .' etc.
4. Then explain how to destroy the blackboard, after reading the messages over a few times and rejecting them. When he's calmed down again, tell him to write his positive thoughts on the white board: 'I enjoy my lessons. . .' 'I find the subject interesting. . .' 'I do my homework and learn what I've been taught. . .' etc.
5. Teach the child to contemplate the white board with a sense of approval and satisfaction. Tell him that it would be a good idea to do this exercise once a day.

You can, of course, use the technique to resolve a host of other problems.

SUGGEST POSITIVE IMAGES

As we've already said, children have no problem visualizing. Exploit this inherent potential by suggesting positive mental self images. For example, if you want to cure your child of bedwetting, teach him or her to visualize positive scenes regularly.

- When he gets up in the morning, the bed is dry. You come into the room and praise him.

- When he asks permission to spend the weekend with a friend, you agree readily because you know he won't wet the bed.
- You give him a set of pretty-coloured sheets because you know he won't ruin them by wetting the bed at night. . . etc.

Suggest that he continues doing these little visualizations every day, once a day – for example when he goes to bed. You may have to wait a few weeks to see some real improvement, but persevere and encourage the child to do the same.

What to Do if Your Child is Ill

Your child has the same capacity as you for participating in his or her own recovery. Teach him the fountain of health exercise, for example, as well as the battle and purification exercises described in Chapter 16. If he has a favourite hero, as most children do, suggest that he solicit his hero's help in fighting harmful microbes.

Explain the illness and the effects of the treatment through concrete, detailed images. If you don't feel sure enough of your knowledge, ask a doctor for help.

You will notice that your child has no difficulty imagining the victorious massacre of the microscopic enemies by his natural defence forces. Don't tell yourself: 'He's too young, he could never understand what's going on inside his body. . .' etc. If you or the doctor take the time to explain clearly what is going on, the child will understand and enthusiastically participate in his recovery. We often commit the error of underestimating our children's ability to understand things.

Don't forget, either, that today's children are much more aware of the exterior world than we were at their age. So don't think: 'At their age I couldn't have understood what a bacterium or a leucocyte is.' What was true for you is no longer true for them.

How to Help a Nervous Child Relax

Most children suffer from anxiety and are over-nervous. Very early on in life they are exposed to stress which can severely upset their digestion and sleep. And the more tension the adults in the family have to deal with, the more the children feel it. So in the same way that you learnt to relax to get rid of the toxins of daily life, you should teach your children to free themselves of their nervousness.

Get comfortable together in a warm, dimly lit room, and set up a relaxation session where you play the role of monitor. Speak softly and confidently. Your child will collaborate willingly.

It's possible that the child becomes so relaxed he falls asleep. If so, take advantage of this special situation to make suggestions, as you learnt to do in the first part of this chapter.

If you teach your children to relax regularly, you will soon notice that nightmares and stomach aches become the rare exception rather than the rule. And in addition, you will have given them the marvellous gift of a healthy and effective habit that they can continue practising for the rest of their lives.

Conclusion

One sentence is sufficient to sum up the principle of this method: 'We reap what we sow.'

Each thought forms one of the innumerable bricks, piled one on top of the other, which constitute our future. Through our acts and feelings, we create the situations we live through. You, not luck or chance, control the natural defences of your body. Through your ideas and feelings, you are capable of strengthening your immune system, and giving it the power to fight for you. Therefore, from now on start to reshape your thoughts and change your attitudes. Banish hate, disdain, jealousy and envy from your mind. Get rid of the gangrene of negativity that is eating away at your health and wellbeing. Open the door to life, happiness, love, friendship and forgiveness. Build yourself a mental sanctuary and use it to regenerate yourself regularly. Fight against the stress that seeps into every corner of our existence and causes so much harm.

And finally – take pleasure in the smallest moment of peace and tranquillity that life offers you. Use those moments to fill yourself with vital life-giving energy, which is the secret ingredient of all health and happiness.

Bibliography

Achterberg, J, *Imagery in Healing* (Shambhala Publications)

Appleton, Nancy, *Lick the Sugar Habit* (Avery Publishing Group, Inc)

Asistent, Niro Markoff, *Why I Survive AIDS* (Simon & Schuster/ Fireside)

Brown, Barbara, *Supermind: The Ultimate Energy* (Bantam)

Carrell, Dr Alexis, *Unknown Man* (Catholic Art Society)

Cousins, Norman *The Will To Be Cured* (Anatomy of an Illness) (Bantam)

Godefroy, Christian H, *La Dynamique Mentale* (Robert Laffont)

Jackson, Dr Arthur, *Stress Control through Self-Hypnosis* (Piatkus Books)

LeShan, Lawrence, *How to Meditate* (Bantam)

Maltz, Maxwell, *Psycho-Cybernetics* (Wilshire)

Oyle, Irwin, *Healing Mind* (Celestial Arts)

Proto, Louis, *Increase Your Energy, Self-Healing* (Piatkus Books)

Simonton, Carl, *Getting Well Again* (Bantam)

Index

Piatkus Books

If you are interested in health, recovery and personal growth, you may like to read other titles published by Piatkus.

Health

Acupressure: How to cure common ailments the natural way   Michael Reed Gach

The Alexander Technique: How it can help you   Liz Hodgkinson

Aromatherapy: The encyclopedia of plants and oils and how they help you   Danièle Ryman

Arthritis Relief at Your Fingertips: How to use acupressure massage to ease your aches and pains   Michael Reed Gach

The Encyclopedia of Alternative Health Care: The complete guide to choices in healing   Kristin Olsen

Herbal Remedies: The complete guide to natural healing   Jill Nice

Hypnosis Regression Therapy: How reliving early experiences can improve your life   Ursula Markham

Increase Your Energy: Regain your zest for life the natural way   Louis Proto

Infertility: Modern treatments and the issues they raise   Maggie Jones

Nervous Breakdown: What is it? What causes it? Who will help?   Jenny Cozens

Psycho-Regression: A new system for healing and personal growth   Dr Francesca Rossetti

The Reflexology Handbook: A complete guide   Laura Norman and Thomas Cowan

Self-Healing: How to use your mind to heal your body   Louis Proto

The Shiatsu Workbook: A beginner's guide   Nigel Dawes

Spiritual Healing: All you need to know   Liz Hodgkinson

Super Health: How to control your body's natural defences   Christian H. Godefroy

Super Massage: Simple techniques for instant relaxation   Gordon Inkeles

The Three Minute Meditator   David Harp

Women's Cancers: The treatment options   Donna Dawson

Recovery

Adult Children of Divorce: How to achieve happier relationships   Dr Edward W. Beal and Gloria Hochman (Foreword by Zelda West-Meads of *RELATE*)

At My Father's Wedding: Reclaiming our true masculinity   John Lee

Children of Alcoholics: How a parent's drinking can affect your life   David Stafford

The Chosen Child Syndrome: What to do when a parent's love rules your life   Dr Patricia Love and Jo Robinson

Codependents' Guide to the Twelve Steps: How to understand and follow a recovery programme   Melody Beattie

Codependency: How to break free and live your own life   David Stafford and Liz Hodgkinson

Don't Call it Love: Recovery from sexual addiction   Dr Patrick Carnes

Homecoming: Reclaiming and championing your inner child   John Bradshaw

Obsessive Love: How to free your emotions and live again   Liz Hodgkinson

When Food is Love: Exploring the relationship between eating and intimacy   Geneen Roth

Personal Growth

Be Your Own Best Friend: How to achieve greater self-esteem and happiness   Louis Proto

Care of the Soul: How to add depth and meaning to your everyday life   Thomas Moore

Colour Your Life: Discover your true personality through colour   Howard and Dorothy Sun

Creating Abundance: How to bring wealth and fulfilment into your life   Andrew Ferguson

Dare to Connect: How to create confidence, trust and loving relationships   Susan Jeffers

Fire in the Belly: On being a man   Sam Keen

Living Magically: A new vision of reality   Gill Edwards

The Passion Paradox: What to do when one person loves more than the other   Dr Dean C. Delis with Cassandra Phillips

Protect Yourself: How to be safe on the streets, in the home, at work, when travelling   Jessica Davies

The Power of Gems and Crystals: How they transform your life   Soozi Holbeche

The Power of Your Dreams   Soozi Holbeche

The Right to be Yourself: How to be assertive and make changes in your life   Tobe Aleksander

For a free brochure with further information on our range of titles, please write to:

Piatkus Books
Freepost 7 (WD 4505)
London W1E 4EZ

PIATKUS

INCREASE YOUR ENERGY
by Louis Proto

In this book, Louis Proto recommends a complete programme
which will help you to overcome fatigue in a natural way,
leaving you with increased energy levels and a greater sense of
vitality. He shows you how to:

- Improve your diet and nourish yourself correctly
- Recharge your batteries when you are feeling drained
- Centre and ground your energy, using breathing, yoga and
  meditation
- Transform your energy from negative to positive and deal
  with anger and stress
- Be more aware of the energy you are putting into
  relationships

Louis Proto is a well-known author, counsellor and holistic
therapist, and an expert in relaxation and meditation
techniques.

SELF-HEALING
by Louis Proto

In *Self-Healing*, Louis Proto explains clearly and concisely how
you can use your mind to heal your body, improve the quality of
your life, and enjoy greater wellbeing. This fascinating book
shows you how you can:

- Develop a positive mental attitude to help fight illness
- Use visualisation and affirmations to make yourself better
- Eat the foods which detoxify your body and strengthen your
  immune system
- Combine orthodox and alternative medicine

Louis Proto is a well-known author, and was for many years a
counsellor and holistic therapist.

THE ENCYCLOPEDIA OF ALTERNATIVE HEALTH CARE
by Kristin Olsen

The Encyclopedia of Alternative Health Care is a comprehensive guide to holistic health care and complementary medicine. It explains:

- Over 30 therapies, including Acupressure, Chiropractic, Iridology, Reflexology, Rolfing, T'ai Chi and Traditional Chinese Medicine
- What each therapy can and cannot do
- The theory and science behind each therapy

Packed with information, *The Encyclopedia of Alternative Health Care* will open the way to a new level of wellbeing. Kristin Olsen is a journalist, health educator and private consultant who has been investigating various healing arts for many years.

THE REFLEXOLOGY HANDBOOK
by Laura Norman with Thomas Cowan

With hundreds of clear diagrams, drawings and charts, *The Reflexology Handbook* explains how you can use this easily accessible holistic treatment to relieve a wide range of physical problems. It shows how:

- Foot reflexology can relieve common conditions such as headaches, respiratory ailments, osteoporosis, sports injuries, insomnia, high blood pressure and weight problems
- Reflexology can reduce stress and revitalise energy

Laura Norman is one of America's top reflexologists. She has been a practising reflexologist for over 20 years and runs her own centre in New York.

ACUPRESSURE
by Michael Reed Gach

Acupressure is an ancient healing art. Safe and easy to learn, with no drug-induced side effects, acupressure is an excellent way to complement conventional medical care. The book includes:

- Simple techniques to relieve over 40 health problems, such as headaches, arthritis, colds, fatigue, insomnia, backache and depression
- Pressure point diagrams and exercises to relieve pain
- A 5-minute acupressure routine to maintain health and relieve stress
- Over 400 photographs and line drawings

Michael Reed Gach is the founder and director of the Acupressure Institute of America. He has been promoting self-healing and wellness through acupressure for over 15 years.

THE SHIATSU WORKBOOK
by Nigel Dawes

The Shiatsu Workbook shows how you can use this ancient healing art to promote healing, health and wellbeing in others. It contains all the background information you will require and shows you clearly and simply how to give your partner a full body treatment. Illustrated throughout, with easy-to-follow instructions, it is the ideal book for everybody who is interested in shiatsu. Discover how shiatsu can be used:

- As a preventive treatment for many everyday ailments
- To reduce stress
- To strengthen the mind, spirit and libido
- To aid the digestive system
- To improve posture and overcome back problems
- And much more

Nigel Dawes has studied shiatsu in Japan, China, Thailand and Korea. He runs The London College of Shiatsu.

AROMATHERAPY
by Danièle Ryman

Aromatherapy is packed with advice on using essential oils and plants to heal minor ailments and promote good health. It includes:

- A comprehensive A–Z of plants and their essential oils
- Information on how each oil or plant can be used in aromatherapy
- An A–Z of over 100 everyday ailments and how they can be treated
- Safety advice
- Recipes for lotions, massage oils and tisanes
- Advice on how aromatherapy can be used in your diet

Danièle Ryman is the world's leading authority on aromatherapy and this book is a distillation of all her skills, experience and research.

HERBAL REMEDIES
by Jill Nice

Herbal Remedies shows you how to use the curative power of plants and herbs to treat common ailments safely at home, without resorting to drugs. In addition it shows how herbs can be used to prevent illness and promote wellbeing. It includes:

- An A–Z of ailments, for quick and easy reference
- Useful information on symptoms and causes
- Tried and tested remedies
- Fascinating descriptions of treatments over the centuries
- Recipes for natural cosmetics and herbal preparations to scent and purify the home

Jill Nice is a respected authority on preparing herbal medicines and has run her own highly successful herbal remedies and cosmetics business.

HYPNOSIS REGRESSION THERAPY –
AND HOW IT CAN HELP YOU
by Ursula Markham

Hypnosis Regression Therapy – and How It Can Help You
answers the questions you may have concerning this increasingly
popular therapy. Discover:

- What hypnosis regression therapy is
- How it works
- When it can be used
- If it's right for you

Ursula Markham is one of Britain's most respected
hypnotherapists. With the aid of case histories she looks at the
problems – such as anxiety, low self-esteem, phobias, depression,
impotence, weight, stammering – that can be successfully
overcome and shows you how you too can benefit.

THE POWER OF YOUR DREAMS
by Soozi Holbeche

The Power of Your Dreams is based on Soozi Holbeche's
experiences of dream work and is an extraordinary guide to our
powerful inner world. Using dozens of examples from her own
dreams and from her therapy sessions, Soozi explains how our
dreams have the power to prophesy, heal, warn, empower and
guide. Discover how to:

- Use dreams as a pathway to the unconscious
- Incubate dreams and ask for help and insight
- Recall your dreams and interpret them
- Use dreams to make positive and healing changes in your life

Soozi Holbeche is a dream therapist and healer. Her previous
book, *The Power of Gems and Crystals,* has become a bestseller
in its field.

NERVOUS BREAKDOWN
by Jenny Cozens

In this book Jenny Cozens sets out to dispel the ignorance and mystery that surround the term 'nervous breakdown'. She helps you to identify the problems and pressures which are ruining your life or the life of someone you know. Whether you are suffering from stress, phobia, anxiety, depression, eating disorder, alcohol addiction or schizophrenia, *Nervous Breakdown* discusses the signs which show you that things are going wrong, and describes the types of help which are available.

Dr Jenny Cozens is a Chartered Clinical Psychologist. She lectures at the University of Leeds, writes a regular advice page and articles for *Good Housekeeping* magazine and is a frequent broadcaster on radio and television.

THE THREE MINUTE MEDITATOR
by David Harp

The Three Minute Meditator introduces you to 30 simple and quick ways to unwind your mind anywhere, and at any time. David Harp's easy techniques will show you how to:

- Get rid of tension
- Learn to relax
- Diffuse anger
- Build self acceptance
- Deal with fears and phobias
- Cope with loss and grief
- Overcome feelings of loneliness

In *The Three Minute Meditator,* David Harp suggests exercises and meditations which will help you to control your mind so that it works for you, and not against you. Meditation is the perfect way for you to achieve inner peace and greater wellbeing.

BE YOUR OWN BEST FRIEND
by Louis Proto

The best route to happiness is to learn how to feel good about yourself and increase your self-esteem. This book shows you how to love yourself unconditionally, for who you are.

- Learn how to use affirmations, visualisations and meditation techniques to enrich your life
- Find out how to nourish yourself better, from within and without
- Discover how love can heal
- Learn how to take responsibility and not be a victim
- Find out how to accept yourself, 'warts and all'

Louis Proto is a well-known author, and was for many years a counsellor and holistic therapist.

CARE OF THE SOUL
by Thomas Moore

Care of the Soul is an inspirational guide that examines the connections between spirituality and the problems of individuals and society. It offers a new way of thinking about daily life – its problems and its creative opportunities. Thomas Moore presents a therapeutic programme for bringing the soul and spirituality back into your life, and shows you how to look more deeply into emotional problems and sense sacredness in ordinary things – real friends, satisfying conversation, fulfilling work, and experiences that stay in the memory and touch the heart.

Thomas Moore is a Jungian psychotherapist, lecturer and writer in the areas of archetypal and Jungian psychology, mythology, religion and the arts.

PSYCHO-REGRESSION: A NEW SYSTEM FOR HEALING AND PERSONAL GROWTH
by Dr Francesca Rossetti

In the 1990s past-life therapy is becoming recognised as a successful way to discover why people feel and act as they do. Francesca Rossetti's unique system of Psycho-Regression healing helps people to find the cause of problems which may have their roots in lives lived hundreds or thousands of years ago. Psycho-Regression takes you back to the source of the negativity that continues to cause problems in your life, and releases it so that positive energy and healing can flood in and bring you increased vitality, creativity and spiritual growth. This book is for anyone who wants to increase their awareness about their spiritual roots and bring about inner change as well as for anyone suffering from specific fears, phobias, unhappy relationships or recurrent problems of any kind.

Dr Rossetti has been a practising past-life therapist for over 20 years. She is also a researcher into the paranormal aspects of the human psyche and a spiritual teacher.

HOMECOMING: RECLAIMING AND CHAMPIONING YOUR INNER CHILD
by John Bradshaw

John Bradshaw is a major figure in the field of recovery and dysfunctional families. His 'inner child' work is a powerful, new therapeutic tool. The people who come to his workshops bring with them persistent problems such as addiction, depression, troubled relationships and chronic dissatisfaction. He helps them to reach back to the source of their problems – their childhood and adolescence – and understand how the wounds received then can continue to contaminate their adult lives. He offers them the chance to reclaim and nurture their 'inner child' and grow up again. This experience has transformed their lives. Reading this book will help you to transform your life and find a new joy and energy in living.